WHY DO YOU KILL?

JÜRGEN TODENHÖFER

Published by:
The Disinformation Company Ltd.
163 Third Avenue, Suite 108
New York, NY 10003
Tel.: +1.212.691.1605
Fax: +1.212.691.1606
www.disinfo.com

First published in Germany by C. Bertelsmann as *Warum tötest du, Zaid?*

Library of Congress Control Number: 2009921366

ISBN: 978-1-934708-14-9

Design & Layout: Greg Stadnyk

Managing Editor: Ralph Bernardo

Distributed by:
Consortium Book Sales and Distribution
Toll Free: +1.800.283.3572
Local: +1.651.221.9035
Fax: +1.651.221.0124
www.cbsd.com

Printed in the United States of America

10 9 8 7 6 5 4 3 2 1

WHY DO YOU KILL?

The Untold Story of the Iraqi Resistance

JÜRGEN TODENHÖFER

disinformation

Table of Contents

Dedicated to the people of Iraq
and all the wretched of this earth

Foreword

by Anthony Arnove

For the United States, we are all terrorists. They don't
distinguish between terrorists who murder civilians and
genuine resistance fighters, who are fighting to liberate their
country. They have no idea about our dreams or our suffering.
In their view, we are worthless.

ZAID, RESISTANCE FIGHTER

For all the talk we have heard about "liberating Iraq," it is remarkable how much contempt in reality the U.S. government has shown to their supposed Iraqi beneficiaries, whose opinions, ideas, values, feelings, and rights are routinely ignored.

Jürgen Todenhöfer rightly points out this hypocrisy (commenting that more generally "Western policies towards the Muslim world suffer from a shocking ignorance of even the simplest facts"). At great personal risk, he sought, as an unembedded writer, to find the stories of Iraqis whose voices have been so systematically excluded from discussion among policy planners and the establishment media. They are voices we should pay attention to and that have much to teach us.

In *1984*, George Orwell described a world in which words

meant their opposite. It is usually understood he was writing about the Soviet Union. But Orwell was describing not just the behavior of the Soviet Empire, which often could rely on brute force to achieve its program of suppressing popular participation in the society, but Western capitalist countries that relied more fully on propaganda and control of information to suppress democracy.

We inevitably enter such an Orwellian world the moment we discuss Iraq.

In the establishment media, it is taken for granted we are "bringing democracy" to Iraq. Some commentators think this was a good idea, but poorly executed. Others think it was a good idea, but maybe overly ambitious. (We underestimated how "depraved" the Iraqis were, as one supporter of the war noted, explaining why the occupation had not gone according to plan.) Some think this is a bad idea. (We must recognize that, despite all our best intentions, Arabs or Muslims are not ready for democracy, they explain with their sober realism.) One can argue over the tactics of the war, its conduct, the degree of "soft" or "hard" power that should be used, whether waterboarding is or is not torture, and so on, but one cannot question the fundamental premise that we are motivated by noble intentions, including the desire to see Iraqis enjoy the benefits of democracy.

To reference the fact that Iraq is at a major crossroad of world energy supplies—of oil and natural gas. To refer to the U.S. desire to set up military bases in Iraq and use these to project power in this geostrategically vital region—and globally. Or to point to the economic and military interests that explain U.S. policy in Iraq and the Middle East. All of this is to engage in "conspiracy theories."

Even more out of bounds is to ask a simple question: what kind of democracy is it in which, after being invaded on false pretexts, and subjected to years of colonial occupation, the desire of the vast majority of the population, is irrelevant? Poll after poll, including polling done by the U.S. government and military analysts it has employed, as well as allied governments, such as Great Britain's, has shown clearly that the Iraqi people want U.S. forces to withdraw completely—most choosing "immediately" over other options for a timetable or conditions on that withdrawal.

But truly to go beyond the pale is to ask another question: if we did invade Iraq on false pretenses, if we are occupying their country, if we are unwanted by the Iraqi people, don't they have a legitimate right to resist the occupation?

The answer would certainly be yes if the U.S. or any of its allies were subjected to such treatment. Anyone who resisted would be justified and would be a "freedom fighter." But the moment the occupier is an ally—or, more importantly, ourselves—the person who resists us is a "terrorist."

In this worldview, we should be clear, there is no legitimate resistance. The corporate media like to trace the obscene levels of violence in Iraq to Sunni and Shia conflict, "ancient" sectarian hatreds, the role of Al-Qaeda of Mesopotamia, and anything that would deflect attention from its roots in the U.S. invasion and occupation. But we should remember that only one month into the occupation, U.S. troops fired on a peaceful demonstration of Iraqis upset by troops taking over a local school in Falluja, killing fifteen people and wounding 65. "We won't remain quiet over this," Ahmad Hussein, whose son was shot, said at the time.

"Either they [the occupiers] leave Falluja or we will make them leave."

The U.S. response was to crush nonviolent resistance with force—and then attack Iraqis for using "violence" to achieve their aims.

Of course, even these aims could not be honestly discussed, let alone deemed legitimate. The aim of liberating Iraq from foreign occupation became twisted into a desire of Iraqis to restore the Baathist dictatorship of Saddam Hussein. Never mind that many Iraqis repeatedly made clear that they hated Saddam Hussein and the occupation equally (or that it was the U.S. government that backed, armed, funded, and politically defended Hussein as he carried out the worst of his crimes against the Iraqi people, the Kurds, and the people of Iran).

Meanwhile, while fueling a murderous civil war, using classic divide and rule tactics, U.S. military planners explained that we could not withdraw from Iraq because we had to prevent a civil war from breaking out.

Today, even this completely distorted picture of Iraq is slipping farther and farther from our consciousness. Corporate news coverage of Iraq, as bad as it has been, is dwindling. The TV networks have closed their bureaus in Iraq. We are hearing more and more "good news" about how safe it is in Iraq, how the troops are coming home.

The reality is different. Violence has declined from its worst heights but only in a grim illustration of the trend economists call the point of diminishing returns. So much ethnic cleansing and violence has taken place in Iraq that the rate of violence could not continue. It has instead settled into a horrible stasis, marked by institutionalization of ethnic cleansing, mass dispossession (with more than two million Iraqis internally displaced and more than two million driven entirely from the country), and ongoing deprivation for the majority of Iraqis, who lack access to safe drinking water, electricity, or adequate health care.

And, a close look at the fine print on President Barack Obama's "withdrawal" plan shows that it is in reality a redeployment plan. Obama's plan—which he says he will revise based on advice from his military advisers and conditions on the ground—would still leave tens of thousands of troops in Iraq, as well as private contractors, including mercenaries, at least into the year 2010 and most likely beyond. The new Status of Forces Agreement between the United States and the government it installed and helps maintain in power in Iraq will almost certainly be revised to allow some U.S. troops to remain as "trainers." Troops currently labeled "combat troops" will remain but become "non-combat" troops overnight through a verbal slight of hand. And the U.S. will also fight to retain its presence. The U.S. government has built the world's largest embassy in Baghdad. Talk of "permanent bases" is a smokescreen. Technically the United States has no actual "permanent" military bases anywhere, even ones that have been in place for decades.

The modern history of Iraq has been a tragedy in many acts. But it is not a tragedy that has seen its final scene. What exactly its future will be depends on whether we act to compel our government to bring a complete and unconditional end to the occupation, whether we can achieve reparations for the Iraqi people for the immense harm and suffering our invasion has caused, and ultimately on whether we can transform the root causes of the empire. The fate of the Iraqi people, who Jürgen Todenhöfer has bravely given voice to in this book, of the people of the United States, and of the world depends on it.

Anthony Arnove is the author of *Iraq: The Logic of Withdrawal* (Metropolitan Books, 2007) and editor of *Iraq Under Siege: The Deadly Impact of Sanctions and War* (South End Press, 2003).

Resist not against the face of the mighty, and do not strive against the stream of the river. Strive for justice for thy soul, and even unto death fight for justice, and God will overthrow thy enemies for thee.

(JESUS SIRACH 4, 27 F.) OLD TESTAMENT

Searching for the Truth:
A Somewhat Different Introduction

7 Cheswan 5768 (Jewish calendar)
29 October 2007 (Christian calendar)
17 Shawwal 1428 (Islamic calendar)

"Ismahooli—Listen!" cries out the little old storyteller in the al-Nafurah teahouse in Damascus as he slams down his thick sword on a black metal stool. Some of the guests wince, most just shuffle their chairs with a laugh. Dusk has arrived in Damascus, the lights are going on all around the city. Also in al-Nafurah.

The teahouse is located in the shadow of the 1,300-year-old Ummayad Mosque, near the burial place of Saladin, one of the greatest Muslim heroes. Every last seat in this quaint establishment is taken. Syrians of all ages—but also a few tourists from France and England—are drinking small glasses of black tea flavored with peppermint leaves.

In front of a wooden wall opposite the main entrance, Abu Shadi, the storyteller of Damascus, sits in a green-red-and-gold painted wooden chair positioned on a small podium. He is allegedly the last real *hakawati* of the Arabic world. In line with the old traditions of his country, he is dressed in a light gray *saderiah*, a kind of frock, with a shirt and a pair of wide, flowing pants of the same color. A 15 cm-wide, red and silver patterned cummerbund is stretched across his belly. On his head he wears a red fez, called a *tarbouch* in Syria, which lends his crinkled face a sublime touch.

"Ismahooli!" he calls out a second time and begins to read the age-old legend of the slave Antar Bin Shaddat from a big black book. His loud, melodic voice reverberates through the room. The audience listens attentively to his story, which he embellishes with animated gestures. They smile as they answer the questions he interjects and when he livens up the tale with a mischievous little joke or anecdote.

Abu Shadi often pauses to smile at his audience or at himself. When he does so, his large metal glasses slide down his nose a bit. He later tells me that he got the idea of using anecdotes from Nikita Khrushchev, former General Secretary of the Soviet Communist Party, who used to lighten up his endless speeches with humorous interjections.

Whenever Abu Shadi thinks his guests are not listening attentively enough, he slams his blunt sword on the stool again, and then all eyes and ears are with him once more. The audience enjoys following him on his journey to the past. It is as if he were leading them to a distant wonderland on a magic carpet, far away from the bleakness of everyday life in Syria's capital.

Suddenly the rather unromantic ring of a cell phone issues from the pocket of his shirt, bringing us back to the here and now. Abu Shadi grins as he asks the intruder from the present to call back again later because he is on a very important journey to a far away place. The audience bursts into laughter.

Abu Shadi restores silence again with a bang of his sword and resumes his fairytale journey to the glorious past of Arabia. He continues the story of the slave Antar, who attains freedom after a heroic battle. Is Abu Shadi telling in a way the story of the Arabic people?

Lying in front of me is the manuscript of the book I finished a few days ago. It is the story of a young Iraqi, Zaid, who is also fighting for his freedom and for the freedom of his people. I am not sure if Zaid's story will end as happily as the legend of Antar the slave.

I do not know for sure why I felt compelled to see Abu Shadi, the *hakawati* of Damascus, one more time before handing in the manuscript. Something drew me almost magically to this dimly lit teahouse where I first listened to his story two years ago. I wanted to see the bright eyes of his audience again as he tells of heroic deeds from the far off past.

I like this old man whose father always used to bring him to the cafés where the storytellers spun their magic tales and who dreamed of one day becoming a hakawati himself. He made his childhood dream come true and now he enchants people with his melodic, mischievous voice—he even enchanted me, though I don't understand a word of Arabic. So here I am again sitting in a corner of the al-Nafurah teahouse, smoking a water pipe. But my thoughts are far away. They are with Zaid and his friends.

The history of the Arabs is a history of great victories and grave defeats. In the past 200 years, however, there has not been much to celebrate. The advent of colonialism has set back the Arab world and the entire Muslim civilization.

I witnessed a part of the Arabic tragedy myself as a 20-year-old student when I traveled to the French-occupied Maghreb in 1960, during the Algerian war. I lived with an Arabic family in Algiers. Every night when darkness descended, I felt the people's fear of the war and raids by the French underground movement OAS.

After 10 days in Algiers I took the train to the East of Algeria to the city of Constantine. During the journey I listened for hours as drunken German and English Foreign Legionnaires told of their "heroic exploits." I will never forget one scene in particular:

When the train rolled out of the station in Algiers, a German Legionnaire grabbed a crate of lemonade from a young Arab boy peddling drinks to the train passengers from the platform. The little Algerian boy, perhaps seven years old, began to smile from ear to ear. The Legionnaire leaned the crate on the windowsill with one hand and with the other began to dig for change in his pocket. He took his time. The train started rolling out.

The little boy ran alongside the train and began begging for his money. The Legionnaire just stared at him derisively. As the train moved faster and the boy began to cry, the soldier held the crate up high and laughed: "Voilà ton argent!—Here's your money!"—and dropped the crate of lemonade on the platform.

The bottles broke into a thousand pieces. The boy's sobs were lost in the din of the drunken soldiers' laughter.

One year later, in late July of 1961, I was in the Tunisian city of Bizerte during the Bizerte Crisis.[1] The city was a French military stronghold that played an important role in the Algerian war. Tunisia had been demanding its return since gaining independence in 1956, in vain.

When Tunisian troops blocked the stronghold in 1961, the French air force bombed the city and sent in paratroopers. After heavy fighting, during which the French military shot at unarmed Tunisian demonstrators, the entire civilian population of the city was evacuated. 670 Tunisians were killed and 1,500 wounded.

In order to visit Bizerte, one needed special permission from the French military authorities. I didn't have a permit. Tunisian friends were able to sneak me into the city. I wanted to photograph this badly ravaged ghost town. Unfortunately, I was quickly arrested by the French military police and forced into a Jeep for a rough ride to occupation headquarters. The machine gun pressed into my back made me very nervous.

After several hours of harsh interrogation I was able to leave the city. I was very lucky. I happened to know relatives of the French commander of the city through my studies in Paris. This led to an unexpected favorable turn during the interrogation.

Otherwise I would not have gotten off so easily. In French prisons you could waste away for violating martial law. And colonial prisons didn't have a reputation for being particularly comfortable, either. But I was able to smuggle the photographs out of Bizerte.

Many years later in 1980, as a representative in the German Parliament, I marched with Afghan freedom fighters from Pakistan through the Hindu Kush mountains by foot to Afghanistan. Six months earlier the country had been attacked by Soviet troops. I wanted to get a first hand impression of the situation of the Afghan people and the freedom fighters.

Word of my journey got around—all the way to Moscow, where a diplomatic reception was being held to mark the 10th anniversary of the German-Soviet Friendship Treaty. Leonid Samjatin, the speaker for Soviet General Secretary Leonid Brezhnev, went into a fit of rage in the company of German diplomats. With a red-hot face, he yelled that if I were caught, I would be whipped and then shot.

Nonetheless, I returned to that oppressed country twice, in 1984 and 1989.[*] My reports about the misery of the Afghan people led to the collection of a fund equivalent to 10 million euros

---

[*] The Soviet army had left Afghanistan in February 1989. Their Communist politically and militarily ruled government stayed in office in Afghanistan until 1992, also because the West had nearly completely ended their support for the Afghan freedom fighters. Koelbl, Susanne, Ihlau, Olaf: *Geliebtes, Dunkles Land* (*Loved, Dark Country*). München 2007, p. 24: "The Americans, it seems, have not learned their lessons from Afghan history and Soviet failure. They are caught in the Hindu Kush trap and so are the multinational protection forces of their allies. 'If God wants to punish a nation He lets it invade Afghanistan,' an old Asian proverb says."

today, which went toward Afghan refugees and in particular refugee children. My journeys paid off.

In 1988 I was able to initiate a meeting of the Afghan Government-in-exile in Urgun, a small village high in the mountains on the Afghan side of the Hindu Kush. With jeeps, donkeys and by foot, we made our way through jagged cliffs and torrential mountain streams to reach the tiny village.

At Christmas 2003, President Hamid Karzai smiled as he told me during a private trip to Kabul that he well remembers that first cabinet meeting of the exiled government on Afghan soil. At the time he was assistant to the president of the government, Sibghatullah Mojaddedi.

Before my latest trip to Iraq in the summer of 2007, I had been there three times already. I had come twice before the war with my children Frédéric and Nathalie, and then one year following the war with my friend Belal El Mogaddedi, a nephew of the first post-Communist president of Afghanistan. I wrote about these journeys in my books *Who Would Cry for Abdul and Tanaya?* and *Andy and Marwa*. I simply felt obliged to write these books. One cannot protest against the Soviet invasion of Afghanistan, and remain silent over the U.S. invasions of Afghanistan and Iraq.

I also visited Iran twice in the past two years, a country that is the subject of much controversy. I hope that I will never have to write a book about Iran, and that neither zealots in Tehran nor hawks in Washington will be able to have their way. But it is precisely this precarious situation that makes me want to describe some of my personal impressions of this country.

I made my first trip to Iran in 2005 with my oldest daughter, Valérie, who was then 23 years old. We were often asked by young Iranians, with a smile, how many terrorists we had seen that day. The Bush administration's whole-scale accusation of terrorism and the presumptuous division of the world into Good and Evil is a constant target of ridicule for young Iranians who are otherwise critical of their own government and pro-Western in outlook.

I very much liked the romantic city of Isfahan, which was once the seat of the great Persian dynasties and boasts many graceful mosques and palaces, lovely city squares and bazaars. I was particularly in awe of the Si-o-se Pol Bridge—the 33 Arches Bridge—that spans the Zayandeh River and of the sprawling park along the riverbank.

On sunny afternoons and holidays, the Zayandeh River Park is like Central Park in New York. Thousands of people sit along the bank in groups, talking or picnicking. Sometimes you even see young couples, but their numbers are fewer and they are not as openly passionate as those in Manhattan. Some people come here just to take a nap. Not far from the banks of the Zayandeh, on the picturesque Neqsh-e Jahan Square, horse-drawn coaches line up just like in Central Park.

My daughter Valérie and I were asked again and again by both young and old Iranians where we were from. We sat down with the people who addressed us and after 10 minutes at most, we were invited for dinner the next day. It's a shame that so few Americans travel to the banks of the Zayandeh River and so few Iranians to Central Park. This is particularly true for the leaders of both countries, who are often engaged in reproducing awful nonsense about one another.

Underneath the "Bridge of the 33 Arches," young Iranians meet with each other in the afternoons. They use the fantastic acoustics of this 400-year-old stone bridge for singing old Iranian songs, which reverberate through the arches. Occasionally an old bard will also belt out his song, but this is rather an exception here.

Valérie and I were listening to the ballads of two young Iranians on a fine spring day. I would have liked to sing along. But my daughter let me know that if I did, I would be traveling alone in the future. And they would probably throw me in the river anyway, she added. With a heavy heart I renounced my impulse to join in their song.

Perhaps this was the reason I returned to Isfahan a year later, during the first week of the 2006 soccer world championship. And when a few Iranians, including an older/elderly man, began singing their ballads on the 33 Arches Bridge, I took heart and followed suit with the Volga Song from the Czarevich operetta in German. By the end of my song most of the Iranians listening were humming along. I received a thunder of applause.

It was probably not the best performance of my life, but I will never forget that afternoon in Isfahan. To sing a German aria in the "Axis of Evil" as an Honorary American Colonel—who else can say that he has experienced that?

During my second trip to Iran, the people were again generous hosts. The world soccer championship in Germany was also the number one topic here. Our guide in Tehran argued for hours with our taxi driver over who was going to invite us home to watch the Iran versus Mexico game. The guide pulled the trump card two hours before kick off by simply declaring herself hostess for the evening.

When I asked her whether she is equally as good at asserting herself at home against her husband, she laughed and said things are the same in Iran as everywhere else. The stronger person has the command, and in some marriages that means the man, and in others, the woman. She was not interested in what the Mullahs have to say on the subject, remarking only that even they aren't always allowed a say at home, either.

When I cast her a doubtful glance, she nodded thoughtfully. Particularly in rural areas, the situation for women was still very bad, she said, but that has little to do with Islam. It is rooted in age-old patriarchal customs that existed long before Islam. The fact that many politicians are afraid to tackle the problem is indeed very sad, she concluded.

An hour later at her cozy little house, she was the first to take off her veil and chador. Dressed in jeans and a t-shirt, she prepared a snack for us. After the game (which Iran lost), her husband cleared the table. There was no doubt left who has the final say in that marriage.

Most of the time, we traveled through Iran without a guide. Whenever we inquired on the street about a particular tourist site, we were given a ride to our destination without hesitation. Often our spontaneous host would pay the small entrance fee for us, too.

Only once did I have real trouble during a visit to Iran. When I ignored a sign that said "Photographs forbidden" and began photographing the Iranian Parliament, I was told by a police guard to erase the photos I had taken. I failed miserably in my attempts to explain the absurdity of this demand.

But when I showed the guard that I also had photos of the opening game of the soccer world championship—Germany against Costa Rica—that I had taken at the game a week before, suddenly the man's face lightened up again. We engaged in a lively discussion on who had the best chances of winning the tournament. In the end I was allowed to keep my photos of the Iranian Parliament.

Shortly before our return flight to Germany, we were at Tehran airport where I spotted a woman with a child in her arms, the little girl wearing a small American flag as a headscarf. I had to rub my eyes. Imagine, in the middle of the "axis of evil," in a country George W. Bush had regularly threatened with a preventative military strike, a young Iranian woman choosing to decorate the head of her two-year-old child with the Stars and Stripes!

I was so amazed that I asked the woman whether she didn't fear an admonishment from Iranian security officials or the Revolutionary Guard. She laughed and said that only in Europe are headscarves forbidden. I followed up my question by asking what she thinks of America's policy toward Iran. The young woman pulled another beaming smile. She said America is a wonderful country and the conflict between Iran and the U.S. is a conflict between politicians—and she herself is not interested in politics.

She allowed me to take a few more photos and then disappeared into the crowds with a friendly wave, carrying off her

Stars and Stripes infant. It seemed to me that we were the only ones interested in her child's headscarf.

I have visited Israel three times and it is one of the most beautiful and exciting countries I know. I have been to Tel Aviv and Jerusalem, and I spent many hours filled with grief at the Holocaust museum in Yad Vashem. I spent my afternoons in the Garden of Gethsemane, where a Spanish Franciscan monk named Rafael would open the gate for me. There I finished reading the Old Testament and wrote parts of this book sitting under the shade of ancient olive trees.

High up on the Mount of Olives, there is a centuries-old Jewish cemetery. Right next to it in a lovely olive grove, there is also a small church called the "Dominus Flevit." As the fall of Jerusalem neared, Jesus is said to have wept here. I also spent many hours in this olive grove. When I looked over the ancient tombs, I always thought of Solomon's melancholic words from the Old Testament:

Vanity of vanities, all is vanity. What profit has man in all his toil that he toils under the sun?

(ECCLESIASTES, CHAPTER 1, 2–3)

Again and again I have read these words sitting under "my" olive trees and I have thought about how little I have heeded this advice in my life.

I lost my heart in Jerusalem, in this dreamlike metropolis of Judaism, Christianity and Islam. I will always return to this magical city. It is the most impressive of all the cities I have been to.

During my journeys I also visited the Palestinian areas in Bethlehem, Nablus and Hebron, the city where the tomb of Abraham is located. Gaza is the only place I haven't been to. Very friendly but resolute young Israeli soldiers pointed their machine guns at me and explained that I have no business going to Gaza. And I thought Gaza belonged to the Palestinians.

In Israel and in the Israeli-occupied Palestinian territories, I once again met many wonderful people—endearing, spiritual Israelis and kind, helpful Palestinians. I spent lovely evenings with both peoples of this embattled country. The Israeli-Palestinian problem is less a problem of its people than of the politicians and functionaries on both sides of the conflict. Every time a solution seems in sight, the extremists of both sides sabotage the opportunity. This blind mechanism seems to be almost inevitable.

In my earlier profession as a spokesman for the CDU/CSU on development aid and arms control, I frequently traveled during the course of my work. And after my time in politics, I still spent almost every vacation and almost every long weekend traveling the world. I found it more interesting to explore foreign countries than to lie in the sun on an overcrowded beach. I learned a lot on these journeys. Again and again I found I had to correct my own prejudices, although I had always thought prejudices were something only other people had.

Equally as fascinating as my travels to other countries were the "journeys" I took through the 1,800 small-printed pages of the Bible and the 520 pages of the Qur'an. This may come as a surprise. But I have never read a more exciting, beautifully written book than the Old Testament, nor a book so full of love than the New Testament, nor a book more infused with the spirit of justice than the Qur'an—the poetic brilliance of which still shines through even in the poorest of translations.

I recommend these three master works of world literature and world history to everyone—above all to those politicians who are constantly talking about them without ever having read them. Anyone who reads these enthralling, majestic works will understand why they have influenced and continue to influence the world so much.

I love the Arabic world, but I also like to travel to other regions. I have visited Latin America, Cuba, and Chile. I traveled to Mozambique and Angola during their independence wars; and I have traveled extensively in Asia, most recently to Laos, Cambodia, and Vietnam.

I have also been to the Soviet Union, and later Russia, several times—sometimes as an official guest of state. Even there, among high-ranking Communists, decorated generals and field marshals, I met many people who impressed me immensely—despite the fact that I was and still am an adamant opponent of Soviet Communism. Ultimately, it is not as easy to divide the world into black and white, or good and evil, as many people have imagined—including me in my younger days.

But more than anywhere else I have traveled to the United States, where I have many friends. I have often been to the Pentagon, the Capitol, and the White House. Many leading and still active U.S. politicians have received me personally. Two of my children have studied in the U.S. I regret that I never had the opportunity to study there myself. The United States was, and still is, a wonderful country.

Some of my journeys were very difficult. During my first march over the Hindu Kush and through the cragged deserts of Afghanistan, I lost fifteen pounds. There was nothing heroic about this trip. My body was covered with fleabites and mosquito bites, and I looked miserable. Journeys like that only become heroic in hindsight, when you reminisce about them while sitting by a warm fireplace.

I am often asked why I always undertake such difficult trips. It is something I can't explain myself. One of the reasons may have to do with the fact that as a child, I had an almost detective-like urge to find out the truth of things—the truth behind all the innocuous-sounding statements and communiqués issued by those in power and their PR machines. The truth, I discovered, can only be found on the street and not in front of the television.

In 1945, the final year of the war, when Germany was being bombed frequently, I was a four-year-old boy living in Burgallee, on the outskirts of the city of Hanau. During the nights of the air raids, I drove my mother almost mad because I always wanted to dash outside and explore the streets after a bombing to search for grenades and bomb shards. I collected the ones that were still warm. Despite the inevitable spanking I received after these nighttime excursions, I was always very proud of my box of grenade and bomb remnants.

Ever since childhood, I have not had much respect for authority and those who hold it. A few years ago my father told me that back in 1946 the neighbors rang the bell at our house in Hanau and told us something terrible was happening outside on our street.

Full of fear, my parents ran out to the street through our small garden. There they saw a long column of rattling and squeaking tanks coming our way from the city center. Right in front of our house the tanks took a right turn onto an unpaved walkway. After 10 meters they swerved left again to return to the street. Apparently some obstacle was in their way that forced them off course.

Suddenly my parents saw that the obstacle was in fact me. The tanks had interrupted the game I was playing with my friends, and I had simply laid down in the middle of the street in protest. Lying on my back, I saw how these powerful war machines were forced to create a path of least resistance around me.

I was very happy with the success of my stunt, but my parents were not. Their faces turned pale as they pulled me from the street back into the house. I had to promise them that I would never again lie down in front of a moving tank. But this time I didn't receive a spanking. My parents were too distraught even for that.

My lack of respect for authority, my childish belief in justice, and my equally naïve need to find out the truth—even in war situations—have stayed with me throughout my life. I still believe that all we need to do is follow our conscience without compromise, rather than blindly follow those who are in power. And we must always stand up for justice and human rights, even if doing so means going against the current. These ideals have cost/caused me a lot of trouble, but they have also created a lot of good, both, for me as well as for others.

Unfortunately, in our times some politicians do not seem to feel the urge to seek the truth—let alone to seek justice. They know little about the realities of the countries against whom they pass resolutions or are prepared to go to war. It seems as if, with the growth of their power, their ignorance also seems to grow exponentially.

Often, as I have listened to the speeches of top European and American politicians addressing the Muslim world, I have thought to myself, how can it be that men and women in such elaborate positions are disseminating such nonsense about other countries?

I have even found myself feeling ashamed for much of what I have heard being said by German, British or American politicians about Afghanistan, Iran, Syria and Iraq, not to mention Israel and Palestine—especially when I had just returned from one of these countries. Often in these situations I recall the words of Pope Julius III: "Do you not know, with how little wisdom the world is governed?"[2]

In addition, the government PR machines of some Western countries demonstrate an almost inimitable lack of restraint as they spread horror stories about the enemy as a way of gaining the support of their citizens and the rest of the world for their wars of aggression. Big lies are told not only in the so-called "rogue states,"[3] but also in the free nations of the West.

The truth is one of the scarcest commodities in politics. The way the world was misled in the run-up to the Iraq war is just one of countless examples. The sad thing is that the public in the Western world always falls prey to the lies of the warmongers.

The Muslim world is much better informed about us than we are about them. Even the poorest makeshift huts in Iraq or Iran are equipped with a television set. Everyday for hours the people watch not just sports or soap operas, but the news—which is often based on material from the West.

The onslaught of the Internet has also deepened many Muslims' knowledge of the West. During my travels I am again and again amazed at the detailed knowledge of Western foreign policy demonstrated by politically interested Muslims, and I am once again ashamed when they shake their heads in response to the nonsense disseminated by the West about their countries.

The fact that many of my trips were dangerous was something I had to learn to accept. I know that I have a responsibility towards my family and all the people I love. Wherever possible I have tried to avoid risks. And as a faithful Christian, I have a deep trust in God. I believe that the value of a life is not determined by its length, but by its content.

My last trip to Iraq was perhaps the most difficult, besides my trips to Afghanistan. In planning for this Iraq trip, a former Iraqi diplomat and a former German UN official were very helpful. They arranged my contacts with the *al-Muqawama*, the Iraqi resistance.

I asked my contacts to bring me together with representatives of as many different resistance groups as possible. My goal was to gain an overview of the resistance as a whole.* We finalized the remaining details for the trip in May 2007 at meetings in Cairo, Amman and Damascus.

It was clear to me that this trip could be very dangerous. A representative of Al-Qaeda, whom I met in Jordan—I did not know he was a member of Al-Qaeda when I started to interview him—blithely explained to me that I would, of course, be treated as an enemy. Germany was, after all, at war with Muslims in Afghanistan.

During my trip I wanted to find out what is really going on in Iraq today. I wanted to know if the peaceful and kind-hearted people of Iraq I had met on my earlier trips had since turned into bloodthirsty and fanatic terrorists. I wanted to know if the West was really fighting for freedom, democracy and human rights in

---

* Please take a look at the impressive documentary *Meeting Resistance*. The filmmakers, Molly Bingham and Steve Connors, two photojournalists, did their interviews in 2003 and 2004 in Adhamija, a then comparatively quiet, central part of Baghdad. They describe most Americans' mistaken impressions about the Iraqi resistance with the following words: "There are two impressions we seem to have here," Bingham said. "The first one is [that] the majority of violence is against civilians, and they are on the brink of a huge civil war, and the Sunnis and Shias hate each other, and the Americans are standing between these two groups that are just going to kill each other. The next one is that the people fighting against us are some radical fringe group who can be isolated and killed. …The insurgency is mostly ordinary Iraqis."

See also: Wilson, Emily: Iraq's Insurgents Are Ordinary People. *AlterNet*, January 13, 2008, www.alternet.org/story/72984; Jamail, Dahr: The Myth of Sectarian Violence in Iraq. *International Socialist Review*, Issue 57, January/February 2008, www.isreview. org/issues/57/rep-sectarianism.shtml: "Soon after arriving in Iraq in November 2003, I learned that it was considered rude and socially graceless to enquire after an individual's sect. If in ignorance or under compulsion I did pose the question the most common answer I would receive was, 'I am Muslim, and I am Iraqi.' On occasion there were more telling responses like the one I received from an older woman, 'My mother is a Shia and my father a Sunni, so can you tell which half of me is which?' The accompanying smile said it all. Large mixed neighborhoods were the norm in Baghdad. Sunni and Shia prayed in one another's mosques. Secular Iraqis could form lifelong associations with others without overt concern about their chosen sect."

Mesopotamia, the land of the two rivers as some of its leaders claimed to be doing.

I deliberately avoided the "Potemkin villages," the fake settlements established by the Pentagon across Iraq, to convey to journalists escorted around by Humvees a false picture of peace and stability. I had already seen the like in Algeria and Mozambique. It is a standard PR strategy of deception employed by all the occupying forces of this world.

I learned a great deal during these trips. My anger about offensive wars and those who engage in them, but also my anger towards terrorists who kill innocent civilians, has only grown. My outrage at the propaganda machines of Western nations has also grown. They impart/convey to us an image of Iraq that has little to do with the realities of the country.

Since most journalists can only observe the country accompanied by the American military, they are usually only able to see what the PR departments in Washington think they should be allowed to see. And this means they seldom see the truth.

My book is an attempt to provide a view of the other side of the coin. It is thus subjective in perspective. I show how Iraqis speak about the war when there are no heavily armed GIs nearby, and when no helicopters or Humvees have "cleared" and secured the streets for convoys of politicians or the press. This book is an attempt to show what Iraq looks like behind the scenes. I am well aware that this goes against the grain of the past five years in television reporting from Iraq.

My book gives a voice to those who have never been heard by the delegations visiting with Pentagon press officials: the leaders of the Iraqi resistance. It attempts to explain why the resistance is fighting not only against the American occupation, but also against Al-Qaeda terrorists. And it also attempts to delineate the significant differences between freedom fighters and terrorists.

The identities of my interview partners have been altered. I have tried to ensure that they cannot be recognized by anyone. It is important to me to state this explicitly. I want to and must take precautions to make sure that those people who agreed to be interviewed for this book are not harmed. They took a big risk in sharing their stories with me.

Some will criticize me for having met with the Iraqi resistance. I can live with this critique. I am familiar with these reproaches from my travels to French-occupied Algeria and Soviet-occupied Afghanistan. But I am not "anti-American," just as I was never "anti-French" or "anti-Russian."

I am only trying to give voice to those who are desperately fighting for their rights and their freedom. "The wretched of the earth," as the famous anti-colonialist liberation theorist Frantz Fanon called them. And in all three cases—in Algeria in the 1960s, Afghanistan in the 1980s, and Iraq post-2003—it is not the occupying troops who fit this bill, but the legitimate resistance movements.

I am aware that in the West, legitimate freedom fighters who resist the illegal armed occupation are conflated with terrorists who murder civilians. This only demonstrates how little we know about the Iraq war.

But this book is not just about Iraq. The Iraq war is just one chapter in Europe and America's centuries-long policy of aggression toward the Muslim world. I will elaborate on this never-ending story in the afterword.

Finding the appropriate photographs for this book was a long and tedious research endeavor. I have spent entire weekends in front of the computer screen looking through the archives of the major photography agencies. Particularly difficult was the search for images relating to colonialism. The West has cloaked this grim chapter of its foreign policy in darkness.

And so it came that I had to fly once again to Algeria, at Easter 2007, this time to rummage through the vaults in the basements of the museums looking at dusty old magazines and books. The images I found were shocking. I was also confronted with contemporary terrorism: During the week of my stay, Al-Qaeda carried out a brutal suicide attack in Algiers, just a few hundred meters from my hotel. Official sources put the number of dead at 24, with 222 others injured, some of them seriously.[4]

I wrote the most important passages of this book in Al-Jazeera, a district of Ramadi, in Jerusalem and in New York. I wanted to sense the immediate effect of these key places while I wrote. The concluding and final touches to this book were written in Skoura, a small oasis in southern Morocco. Nowhere else does one come so close to the truth as in the desert.

And I spent many weekends in Munich—after a few hours of my favorite pastime, soccer in the English Garden—reviewing what I had written in Iraq, Jerusalem, New York and Skoura and asking myself whether it is appropriate reading material for Western readers. I decided that it is certainly worth a try.

My royalties from this book will be used to help injured Iraqi refugee children and finance a project dedicated to reconciliation between Israelis and Palestinians. This is the key to reconciliation between Muslims, Christians and Jews throughout the world. I firmly believe that reconciliation will come—just as I was one of the few representatives in the German Parliament who believed that East and West Germany would one day be reunited, despite the fact that this idea was not en vogue at the time.

Reconciliation between the Muslim and the non-Muslim world will come one day as well—because it must. This book is intended as a small contribution toward that goal. It is for my children and for your children. Either we shall go down collectively or we shall survive collectively.

"Wa hona ya sadati awdahna alkalam—With these words I end my story," shouts Abu Shadi as he slams down his sword one last time, bringing me back to the present. The story of Antar the slave is over, and the story of Zaid, a young Iraqi, begins.

Whosoever killeth a human being for other than manslaughter
or corruption in the earth, it shall be as if he had killed all
mankind, and whoso saveth the life of one, it shall be as if he
had saved the life of all mankind.

QUR'AN (5:32)

Zaid's Fear

Ramadi, August 2007. "I might as well go straight to Guantánamo and drop my family off in Abu Ghraib! I will not tell you my story."

Zaid is sitting in front of me in the gentle evening sunlight of Ramadi. He is 21 years old and an Iraqi resistance fighter. Zaid is tall and good-looking, with a fine moustache and thick black hair. His eyes are bright, alert and always in motion.

His youthful charm would probably turn the head of many an Iraqi girl, and most probably their mothers as well. But like most young Iraqi men, Zaid does not have a girlfriend. That might have been possible during the Saddam Hussein era, but since his fall the social rules have become stricter. The once secular country has become a state in which the first thing people did was re-introduce antiquated customs and ways, out of fear of Al-Qaeda and the death squads of radical Shi'ite politicians.

Zaid's face clouds over when I ask him to tell me about his life, especially about what he does as a fighter in the resistance, and to show me some photos. He looks at me distantly; his eyes are tired and sad. I sense that in his mind's eye he is reviewing his entire life.

Zaid puts his left hand to his brow and shakes his head: "Then I could buy myself a prison uniform at once. For the United States, we are all terrorists. They don't distinguish between terrorists who murder civilians and genuine resistance fighters, who are fighting to liberate their country. They have no idea about our dreams or our suffering. In their view, we are worthless. If they fail to get me, they will kill all my family instead. Just say that I am fighting in the resistance and that I have lost several family members. I cannot give you any details or photos. Or are you willing to go to Guantánamo in my place?" Zaid has risen. His body language is too obvious to remain unnoticed; it too expresses a most emphatic "no."

I try to explain that I am also taking risks by visiting Iraq. But that does not seem to interest Zaid. "We can trade places anytime," he says coolly, and turns towards the gate of the small garden in which we are sitting.

As he reaches the gate, he turns and says softly, "I will think about it again tonight. And you should think about how you can help my family if something happens to them because of your book." Then he disappears into the dusk of Ramadi.

Journey to the Border

The night before that first meeting with Zaid my alarm clock went off at two o'clock in my hotel room in Damascus. Still half asleep I try to turn it off, but I cannot find it. In the meantime my second alarm clock starts to shrill. I had placed it far from my bed as a precaution.

I give up. I know I have to get up. I plan to set off for the Iraqi border in one hour's time. Two in the morning is a horrible time to get up for someone who loves to sleep in. At home I would roll over and go back to sleep, and then go to the office around nine.

But I know I have to go back to Iraq. Not as an "embedded journalist" with the U.S. occupying forces. I do not want to see the country through the eyes of the occupiers, or from the perspective of a reporter holed up in Baghdad's Green Zone. I want to see Iraq through the eyes of the victims and of the resistance.

One hour later—after downing a large pot of coffee—I am in an old yellow taxi with a wrinkly-looking Syrian driver, who I soon discover does not speak a word of English. I try to tell him I want to go to "Al Tanaf" crossing on the Syrian-Iraqi border.

He turns round in dismay. "Al Tanaf?" he repeats while making a gesture with the edge of his hand crossing his neck that means, "They will cut your throat there!" I reply: "Yes, Al Tanaf! Yallah!" which means: "Let's go!"

The driver shakes his head as we set off. It is just after three in the morning. It is amazing how much traffic is on the roads in Damascus at such an early hour.

The first street traders start to lay out their merchandise on the sidewalks. Butchers, having completed their slaughtering, open their shops. We drive past a Christian church; its brightly illuminated cross shines over the entire neighborhood. We head southeast along Damascus's imposing city wall, which is more than 2,000 years old.

I take the SIM card out of my mobile phone—just in case. The easiest way to locate somebody nowadays is via his cell phone. And nobody needs to know exactly where I am during my stay in Iraq. After 10 kilometers (6.2 miles) we reach the Sayyida Zainab Mosque. Next to its exquisite olive green tiled minarets is an ugly rundown building, and that is where we have to apply for a permit to travel to the Iraqi border. The Syrians do everything they can to make it hard to travel to Iraq. The accusations by the United States administration that Syria supports the Iraqi resistance are having an effect.

We first have to wake up the public servants of the Syrian state, who are sleeping, wrapped in dark blankets, on wooden camp beds in front of the building. With much grumbling and growling they finally issue our permit. When they look at my passport and see that I am German, they shake their head in disbelief. Mumbling something I cannot understand, they hand back my passport and go back to bed. From the mosque, the *muezzin* makes his first call to morning prayers.

At about seven a.m. we reach Al-Shahmma, a godforsaken town 70 kilometers (43.5 miles) from the border. This is where I am to meet Abu Saeed, a trader from Ramadi, who will escort me across the border. Iraqi contacts I had met during Pentecost in Jordan put me in touch with him.

Abu Saeed is waiting for me at the edge of town in a dark blue Chevrolet SUV with tinted windows. With him are his wife Aisha, their 13-year-old daughter Shahla, four-year-old son Ali and his driver Moussa. They had come from Iraq the night before, managing to cross the border just before it closed at 10 p.m. They spent the night together in the SUV.

Abu Saeed speaks English fluently, and we hit it off straightaway. He is 40 years old and with his Iraqi headdress looks like Peter O'Toole in the movie *Lawrence of Arabia*. His wife Aisha, who is also 40, has gentle, almost European facial features. She is a pretty woman, and somehow managed to put on a little make-up in the crowded SUV. I tell her she looks like the great American movie star Rita Hayworth. She thanks me and smiles, although she certainly does not know who that is.

Abu Saeed studied history and originally, he wanted to become a diplomat. Now he owns a small trading company in Al-Jazeera, a quarter of Ramadi. The company deals in construction materials and soft drinks in the Iraq-Syria-Jordan border triangle.

Business is not good, he tells me, but he earns just about enough to look after his family. "We are alive," he says, "that is the most important thing, Alhamdulillah—praise be to God!"

Abu Saeed has four more children, but he left them at home in Ramadi. He only brought his wife, Shahla and Ali along as protection for me, so that our party would look like a family and they might deflect attention from me at checkpoints. Though I am wearing a white Iraqi *dishdasha* that reaches my ankles and a thin moustache, I still look pretty European.

We set off. It is 7:15 a.m.

Our 30-year-old driver Moussa, a quiet Iraqi with a crew cut, drives almost the whole time at top speed. Abu Saeed sits next to him, with his young son Ali on his lap. His wife Aisha and their daughter Shahla have made themselves comfortable in the back. In order not to fall asleep, Moussa keeps playing cassettes of recitations from the Qur'an and fiery sermons. That not only keeps him wide-awake, but me too. Since I don't understand a word of Arabic, I cannot drum up much enthusiasm. Abu Saeed and his family fall asleep at once. They have, after all, had an exhausting night.

After three quarters of an hour driving through the Syrian desert, we are approaching Al-Tanaf. The border post is in reality a five-kilometer long fortress, a sight that triggers memories of the old crossing at Helmstedt between East Germany and West Germany, as well as the Berlin Wall and high-security prisons. It is chilling, nightmarish and oppressive. Nowhere in the old Iraq of Saddam Hussein had I seen such grim looking walls and barriers.

For two hours we drive and walk from checkpoint to checkpoint. Moussa hands out bribes the entire time—sometimes secretly under the cover of the hood, sometimes quite openly through the window. Usually 50 Syrian pounds, equivalent to about one dollar.

Some of the Syrian border police even give change, if one does not have the right bills. One border guard counts his big wad of bills, all bribe money, openly and with evident satisfaction, before giving us a big Syrian Lira banknote as change. Al-Tanaf is well known for its greedy border guards.

Despite the plentiful *baksheesh*, the checks are strict. Abu Saeed says I am a physician from Germany who wants to treat wounded children in Ramadi. But nobody believes him. Why would a German voluntarily go to Ramadi, and without the protection of the U.S. Army?

So we are taken to the official who deals with unusual cases. With a serious expression he tells us that, despite my Syrian and Iraqi visas, I may not enter the country. I would need special permission from the Syrian interior ministry.

We point out that I have a special permit from the Iraqi interior ministry, which is clearly much more important. It had taken me months to get it, and I do not want to believe that after all the hassle it turns out to be worthless! The exchange becomes heated; the official is looking decidedly frosty. Bank notes change hands. They are accepted with thanks. But the official doesn't change his mind.

We insist on speaking to his superior. With a shrug of his shoulders, he agrees. The superior appears, tired and yawning, and Abu Saeed explains to him with fervor how urgently the children of Ramadi need my help. It is only natural for me to want to experience the situation on the ground in Iraq firsthand. Abu Saeed talks and talks.

After a quarter of an hour the official capitulates. He says he has never seen a German come this way to get to Ramadi since the war began. But so be it! "Yallah, go with God, but go!" He leans back in his chair, exhausted. He wants to have his peace of mind and carry on dozing.

One can accuse the Syrians of many things, but not of making

WHY DO YOU KILL?

it easy to get into Iraq. Resistance fighters or terrorists who try to infiltrate Iraq from Syria must have a hard time crossing the border legally. Given the harsh conditions in the desert, to slip across the green border, which drowns here in a sea of yellowish sands, illegally is by any measure a dangerous enterprise. But it must be impossible to monitor every section of the 600-kilometer (373-mile) desert border between Syria and Iraq.

Due to the difficulties obtaining an official visa to Iraq, my contacts and Abu Saeed considered for several weeks whether they could smuggle me into Iraq illegally. But they decided against that option because it would have been too dangerous. And even if I had made it, I would have had no entry stamp in my passport. In Iraq, you can expect to be stopped by police or military at almost every crossroads, so I would have been arrested at the first checkpoint.

At 10:15 a.m.—we are still on Syrian soil—we are allowed to proceed along a slalom course of concrete blocks, sandbags and menacing shooting stands and onto a wide four-lane road. It is lined by high concrete walls and passes through five kilometers of no man's land to the Iraqi border.

To our right, between the road and the concrete wall, we see 50 or 60 pitiful tents bearing the logo of the United Nations refugee agency, UNHCR. This is where a few hundred Palestinians who fled the Iraqi militias have become trapped. They have not fully escaped Iraq and are not welcome in Syria or anywhere else. They endure the searing heat—reduced to nobodies in no man's land.

We approach the Iraqi checkpoints. A sign bearing red letters on a white background greets us: "Do not attempt to cross the stop line or to bribe the border police. Do not enter the desert. Whoever disregards these orders will be arrested, interrogated and jailed."

The prospect of not having to pay bribes in Iraq is delightful, after our experiences in Syria. But the order not to go into the desert is superfluous. Faced with heavily armed control towers, shooting stands and the inhospitable desert, no normal person would for a moment consider such a foray.

By now, the temperature has risen to 118 degrees Fahrenheit. The slalom resumes at a stop-and-go pace around barriers and shooting stands, and past several checkpoints. All around us are masked Iraqi soldiers and heavily armed American security personnel. I can't tell whether they are Blackwater mercenaries, who have been active in ever-greater numbers in the Iraqi security business.

But it does not really matter. Their fingers are resting on the trigger of their submachine guns; the security catches are released. There is clearly no interest in discussions about the meaning and significance of rules and regulations. We have finally arrived in the liberated Iraq.

The atmosphere is grim and threatening. Overlooking the checkpoints with their American security men poised to shoot, there is an observation tower about five or six meters in height. The barrel of a machine gun points menacingly out of a slot in its armored glass cladding.

Again and again I have to get out and, with Abu Saeed's help, explain to the astonished Iraqi border guards why I want to enter their country. Our progress is slow. But we do not have to pay any bribes.

Two hours later, when we have finally persuaded the officials at the last American-Iraqi checkpoint to let us through, an Iraqi police officer who, like all the other border guards, no doubt considers me mad, cheerily calls out:

"Itwanaso zean fil Iraq—Enjoy yourselves in Iraq!" It is 12:30 p.m. now in Syria, and 1:30 p.m. in Iraq.

Journey to Ramadi

It has taken us four and a half hours to get across the border. A big signboard in Arabic welcomes us: "Aliraq Yohibbokom—Iraq loves you." That remains to be seen, I think to myself as I open my third bottle of water for the day. Ahead of us is the highway through the desert to Ramadi, and it is almost empty. How pleasing the open road can be after four hours of stop-and-go. It's just 490 kilometers (305 miles) to Ramadi.

The car's air conditioning is working hard but losing the battle against the enormous heat. Moussa inserts another Qur'an cassette into the player, this time the Sura Abraham, as we speed down the highway at 160 kilometers an hour (100 mph) through the endless desert of Iraq. The road is dead straight and cuts through a barren landscape of sand and stones. The road is lined with thousands of shredded tires that have burst in the heat—which often soars to 122 °F or higher.

Every few kilometers there are burned-out vehicles on the

side of the road. The highway is lined with the twisted wrecks of buses, trucks, cars and military vehicles—pierced by shrapnel, burnished by the sand, whipped up by the fierce desert wind.

Long skid marks, huge oily patches and burn marks on the highway and beside it indicate that attacks, ambushes and battles occurred here not so long ago between American troops and Iraqi insurgents—tragedies with countless dead.

The occupying forces usually send in teams to clear up the scene quickly after battles, to remove evidence of American vulnerability. Here, they tried to move the wrecks as far as possible into the rocky desert. But they could not obliterate all the traces. The asphalt and the desert have a memory of their own.

The road from Al-Tanaf to Ramadi is a car-bomb highway, a highway of death. An explosive device can go off at any moment, or a gun battle can erupt between insurgents and the occupying forces. To the traveler the burned-out wrecks are a constant testimony to this fact.

The journey becomes monotonous, as the same scenes recur: tire shreds, gutted and wrecked vehicles, oil patches, skid marks, desert and more desert and yet more desert—accompanied by verses from the Qur'an and heated sermons blaring out endlessly from the loudspeaker. Occasionally the monotony of the desert is interrupted when herds of sheep suddenly appear out of nowhere. They eat the desert's last meager shoots of grass, which only they can find.

Everyone is asleep, apart from the driver and me. Moussa drives with great calm at top speed, listening to the Qur'an and writing text messages on his mobile phone with his right hand. He can't make phone calls here. The wireless coverage in this huge country is patchy and overstretched.

Suddenly, two helicopters appear, flying low above us. I start to take photos at once. Abu Saeed, who has just woken up, begs me to put my camera away.

All over sudden a column of heavily armored, sand-colored American Humvees and armored personnel carriers appears out of the blue, moving towards us on our side of the road. Bristling with weapons, they are heading right for us. A red warning light is flashing on the roof of the lead vehicle.

Moussa slams on the brakes, throws his cell phone on to Abu Saeed's lap, swerves sharply to the right, and brings the SUV to a screeching halt at the edge of the road. Slowly the convoy of Humvees and tanks gets closer. Everyone in the car is wide-awake now.

I keep taking photos, even though Abu Saeed is yelling at me to stop at once. They shoot at anything suspicious, he says. The American military convoy is just meters away now. The machine guns on the Humvees and the tanks are pointing straight at us. I hide my camera in the net on the back of the driver's seat and wait.

The military vehicles are moving almost at walking speed as they get closer and then pass us by. I look at the faces of the soldiers staring at our vehicle. Abu Saeed is holding his young son tightly in his arms. He is as white as chalk. Then finally, after several minutes that seem like an eternity, they are gone and the scare is over.

Abu Saeed turns to me and says imploringly: "Doctor, please

don't take any more pictures. It is too dangerous. Even through the darkened windows, the GIs can see they are being photographed. And they are quick to shoot."

While Abu Saeed is pleading with me, I notice a convoy of supply vehicles approaching on the opposite lane. It seems to stretch for kilometers. That must be why the military secured our lane and almost forced our Chevrolet into the ditch.

The lead vehicles in the convoy are armored Humvees. And after every six trucks there is an armored personnel carrier or another Humvee. The seemingly endless convoy is apparently headed for Jordan. The neighboring country is a very important source of supplies for the occupying powers in Iraq.

Moussa sets off again very slowly, no faster than the trucks coming the other way. Abu Saeed explains that that is a very important regulation. One has to maintain a distance of at least 150 meters when driving behind a military convoy and may not drive any faster than a convoy coming the other way. Any contravention of these rules is usually fatal—a fact that might explain some of the burned-out vehicles en route. It is 2 p.m., two more hours to Ramadi. The highway is again deserted.

Abu Saeed's Account of the Situation

Abu Saeed plans to introduce me to representatives of the Iraqi resistance over the next few days. I ask him if he belongs to the resistance. He laughs: "We are all members of the resistance, everyone in his own way—directly or indirectly. The people are the resistance. Everybody helps one way or another, as in almost any occupied country. With money, or information, food, shelter—whatever is needed."

He is not a fighter, he tells me, but like all Iraqis he helps in whatever way he can. Though he only supports the "real resistance," and not the "terrorists" of Al-Qaeda or the Shi'ite politicians' militias.

I ask if all Iraqis really do support the resistance. Abu Saeed ponders for a moment: "If you take all of Iraq, including the Kurds, I would say 70 percent of the population certainly support the resistance."

Part of the political class, he continues, has come to terms with the occupiers—but not the people. There is a deep gulf now between the Iraqi government and the Iraqi people. Unlike the members of the government clinging to power, just about the entire population demands the withdrawal of the occupation forces.*

---

* Langer, Gary: What They're Saying in Anbar Province. *New York Times*, September 16, 2007, www.nytimes.com/2007/09/16/opinion/16langer.html: "In a survey conducted Aug. 17–24 for ABC News, the BBC and NHK, ... Seventy-six percent [in Anbar] said the United States should withdraw now [...] every Anbar respondent in our survey opposed the presence of American forces in Iraq—69 percent 'strongly' so. Every Anbar respondent called attacks on coalition forces 'acceptable,' far more than anywhere else in the country. All called the United States-led invasion wrong, including 68 percent who called it 'absolutely wrong.' ... respondents were deeply dissatisfied with the availability of electricity and fuel, jobs, medical care and a host of other elements of daily life."

How questionable the reports about the alleged stabile security situation in the province of Anbar at the moment are, is shown in the number of victims according to the Iraqi Red Crescent Society (IRCS): According to a recent statement by the IRCS for the time period of August to December 2007, the following number of civilian victims for Anbar are available: (bombs, raids, sharp shooters, car bombs, street bombs, etc.): August 2007: 190 deaths; September 2007: 240; October 2007: 245; November 2007: 230; December 2007: 250.

Iraq is like occupied France during the Second World War. Of course there are collaborators, but most people are on the side of the resistance, and feel they are part of the resistance.

"The Shi'ites as well?" I ask. Abu Saeed looks annoyed. The distinction between Sunnis and Shi'ites has been played up by the United States and Britain, he says.[1] In Iraq, nobody used to be interested in who was Sunni and who was Shi'ite. Even in Basra, where almost everybody is Shi'ite, there is a strong national resistance, despite the politicians' powerful militias supported by Iran.

The same Qur'an holds true for both Shi'ites and Sunnis. The only difference worth mentioning is that later, after the death of Muhammad, Shi'ites only accepted descendants of the prophet's family as leaders of the Muslim community. The Sunnis, on the other hand, insisted that the leaders of their community, the caliphs, were to be chosen not on the basis of their descent but their political and religious qualifications. That is what led to the schism.

Abu Saeed enjoys displaying his knowledge of history. He is a Sunni, he continues, his wife a Shi'ite. That is completely normal in Iraq. He has never thought about whether that makes his chil-

---

Not included, according to information by the IRCS, are:

• Victims buried by their families without notifying the Health Department.

• Victims kidnapped from Anbar; their corpses have been found in other provinces, especially in Bagdad.

• Victims from other provinces killed in Anbar, especially those who travelled by car.

• Members of Al-Qaeda or other armed groups found by US-troops in remote desert areas, killed and buried in Anbar.

• Victims within the Iraqi army and police.

dren Sunni or Shi'ite. Even as a student of history, he is not aware of any rules that might apply in such a situation. And, in any case, nobody in Iraq cares. Even many Kurds in Baghdad and Mosul feel they are above all Iraqis, unlike some of their political leaders.[2]

The West's attempt, he continues, to play the Sunnis and Shi'ites off against each other will fail. They are all Muslims. They are proud to be Muslims and Iraqis. Even during the war with Iran, Sunnis and Shi'ites fought side-by-side for years.

After the war with the United States in 1991, there was an uprising in the mainly Shi'ite south. However, it was not, as has often been claimed, an uprising by the Shi'ites against the rule of the Sunnis, but an attempt instigated by the United States and Iran to weaken and, if possible, topple Saddam.

In response, I ask Abu Saeed about the violence between Sunnis and Shi'ites that people around the world see on television every evening. You cannot just argue that away, I say. Abu Saeed retorts that people who blow themselves up in markets or in front of mosques are terrorists and murderers and have nothing to do with the Iraqi resistance.* According to a recent report

---

* Unnamed author: The Kabul resolution to banish suicide attacks as crimes against humanity and Islam. In: Konrad Adenauer Stiftung, Kabul, May 12, 2007, www.kas.de/proj/home/pub/80/1/year-2007/dokument_id-11110/index.html: Qur'an defines *Schahadat* (martyrdom) in 9 Surah of the Qur'an Al-Tauba, Verse 111, where we can read the following: "Allah has bought from the believers their lives and belongings for paradise: They fight for Allah's cause, they kill (during war) and are killed(!)." This means that a fighter who attacks the enemy during war and is mortally injured during this attack, that only this type of death can be understood as Schahadat in the spirit of Islam. This type of death, to be killed by the hands of the enemy, is truly different from suicide or blowing oneself up by mines or other explosives [...]. Qur'an condemns these suicides with the following words in 2 Surah Al-Baqqara, Verse 195: "... do not plunge into your own destruction by your own doings. ... A suicide attack is a crime against Islam and humanity!!!" [Translation]

published on the *Newsweek* website, more than three quarters of suicide bombers come from abroad.[†]

It is a diabolical game, he says, played by Al-Qaeda—funded by so-called charitable foundations in Saudi Arabia and the Gulf states—the militias of Shi'ite politicians—often sponsored by Iran—and the intelligence agencies of certain countries with an interest in seeing Iraq break apart.

All three groups operate in the same way: by means of spectacular attacks they pit different population groups against each other. The Sunni Al-Qaeda attacks Shi'ite holy places and marketplaces; Shi'ite militias attack Sunni holy places and neighborhoods; and foreign agents bomb both Sunnis and Shi'ites—only for their masters to then point in a disdainful mockery at

---

See Surah 2:195: "Spend your wealth for the cause of Allah, and be not cast by your own hands to ruin; and do good. Lo! Allah loveth the beneficent." and Surah 9:111: "Lo! Allah hath bought from the believers their lives and their wealth because the Garden will be theirs: they shall fight in the way of Allah and shall slay and be slain. It is a promise which is binding on Him in the Torah and the Gospel and the Qur'an. Who fulfilleth His covenant better than Allah? Rejoice then in your bargain that ye have made, for that is the supreme triumph."

See also: Grossman, David, p. 122: "Today, and especially at this place, I cannot shake the thought that Samson, in a certain way, was the first suicide bomber [...]. And although the circumstances of his deed were different than the attacks in today's Israel, it is conceivable, that such principle—to seek revenge through suicide and murdering innocents—entered the consciousness of people, such principle that has been perfected so much in recent years." [Translation]

† Unnamed author: The Bombers: A Breakdown: Names and nationalities of known suicide bombers in Iraq. *Newsweek Online*, www.msnbc.msn.com/id/20094235/site/newsweek: "This list contains the names and countries of 139 suicide bombers in Iraq. The bombers came from the following countries: Saudi Arabia (53), Iraq (18), Italy (8), Syria (8), Kuwait (7), Jordan (4), Libya (3), Egypt (3), Tunisia (3), Turkey (3), Belgium (2), France (2), Spain (2), Yemen (3), Lebanon (1), Morocco (1), Britain (1), Bengal (1), Sudan (1) and Unknown (18). (Source: Adapted from 'Suicide Bombers in Iraq' by Mohammed M. Hafez)."

the Iraqis, who evidently "kill each other like savages."

Everybody in Iraq knows, Abu Saeed continues, that foreign agents stage some of the attacks. Even the Shi'ite militia leader Muqtada al-Sadr recently said in public that the attack on the famous Shi'ite Golden Mosque in Samarra[3] in June 2007 was not the work of Iraqi Sunnis but the occupying powers. And that is very interesting, as Muqtada al-Sadr is a protégé of Iran and himself bears responsibility for many attacks on Sunnis.*

When I look at Abu Saeed in disbelief, because it all sounds too much like an Oriental conspiracy theory, he pulls out of his pocket an article from an Arabic-language newspaper that cites that same *Newsweek* report. Reading it out, Abu Saeed says that out of 139 suicide bombers who carried out attacks in Iraq, only 18 were Iraqis, while 53 were from Saudi Arabia, eight were from Italy, two each were from Belgium, France and Spain, and one was from Britain. That means foreigners carried out 87 percent of the suicide bombings on the list. U.S. forces officially confirmed a few

---

* Baker-Hamilton Report (2006), p. 10 f.: "Shiite militias engaging in sectarian violence pose a substantial threat to immediate and long-term stability. These militias are diverse. Some are affiliated with the government, some are highly localized, and some are wholly outside the law. [...] The Mahdi Army, led by Moqtada al-Sadr, may number as many as 60,000 fighters. It has directly challenged U.S. and Iraqi government forces, and it is widely believed to engage in regular violence against Sunni Arab civilians. [...] As the Mahdi Army has grown in size and influence, some elements have moved beyond Sadr's control."

See also: Jamail, Dahr, "The Myth of Sectarianism," *International Socialist Review*, Issue 57, January–February 2008: "U.S.-backed sectarian death squads have become the foremost generator of death in Iraq, even surpassing the U.S. military machine, infamous for its capacity for industrial scale slaughter. It is no secret in Baghdad that the U.S. military would regularly cordon off pro-resistance areas like the al-Adhamiyah neighborhood of Baghdad and allow 'Iraqi police' and 'Iraqi army' personnel, masked in black balaclavas, through their checkpoints to carry out abductions and assassinations in the neighborhood."

days ago that between 80 and 90 percent of suicide attacks were carried out by foreign terrorists.[†]

Abu Saeed has evidently read up on the issue. "Why," he asks me, "are you all taken in by the terrible game the United States and other powers are playing with Iraq? You fell for the lie about weapons of mass destruction, and now you fall for the lie that the suicide bombers are Iraqi. Why are you so susceptible to U.S. propaganda?"

Abu Saeed speaks calmly, but he sounds resigned. "You have no idea what is going on in our country," he adds. For him, al-Zarqawi,[4] the Al-Qaeda leader who was killed in June 2006, furthered the U.S. cause, if unwittingly, by being exactly what the American leadership wanted its ideal enemy to be: brutal, ruthless, and inhuman. That allowed Bush to tell the American people again and again that he had to protect America from such people. In fact, al-Zarqawi, who was Jordanian, killed more Iraqis than any other nationality. Why does nobody write that this murderer was a foreigner and not an Iraqi?

Although all the people of Ramadi have always opposed the American occupation, some tribes agreed to a kind of limited

---

† Unnamed author: Press Conference with Brigadier General Kevin Bergner, spokesman and deputy chief of staff for strategic effects, Multinational Force Iraq; Topic: Operational update; Location: The Combined Press Information Center, Baghdad, Iraq. *Federal News Service*, July, 11 2007: "Al-Qaeda in Iraq is a network led and fuelled by foreign extremists who envision a new caliphate [...] a Taliban-like state [...]. In recent months, more and more Iraqis have begun to reject its extremist ideology and take a stand against them. [...] Approximately 60 to 80 foreigners are lured to Iraq in any given month by Al-Qaeda. Approximately 70 percent transit through Syria [...]. Between 80 and 90 percent of the suicide attacks in Iraq are being carried out by foreign-born Al-Qaeda terrorists [...]."

See also: Rüb, Matthias: Irak-Kämpfer aus Saudi-Arabien (Iraq Fighter from Saudi Arabia). *Frankfurter Allgemeine Zeitung*, November 23, 2007, p. 6.

cease-fire with the Americans a few weeks ago, in order to drive the foreign Al-Qaeda fighters out of town. That has been achieved to a large extent, Abu Saeed continues. Al-Qaeda wanted to make Ramadi its capital, but that attempt has failed.

The population and the resistance simply withheld any support. "As Mao Zedong knew, fish can only live in water. We took away the water, and dried them out."[5] In spring 2007, the foreign Al-Qaeda fighters were finally forced to leave Ramadi.

There weren't any major battles here, just a few local skirmishes involving the Iraqi police, the resistance, the American forces, and Al-Qaeda. The media are blowing these confrontations out of all proportion and reporting them as heroic battles—like the one at Donkey Island[6] near Ramadi, for example, on June 30, 2007, when U.S. units reportedly killed about 30 Al-Qaeda fighters. But these are the kind of gun battles that unfortunately occur in Iraq every day. Al-Qaeda did not fail in Ramadi by losing a battle, but by losing the respect of the population because of its boundless brutality.

The defeat of Al-Qaeda in Ramadi shows, Abu Saeed continues, how peace in Iraq can be restored one day. As soon as the American troops leave, the Iraqi resistance across the country can concentrate on Al-Qaeda and the 100 or more militias, most of which are led by radical Shi'ite politicians, and a few by Sunnis. The resistance would only need a few weeks to solve the problem of terrorism. The Iraqi people would love to be rid of the terrorists.

I look at Abu Saeed skeptically, but he is convinced of his position. The fact that the people of Ramadi drove Al-Qaeda out of town has given him a new sense of optimism.

Slowly, Abu Saeed dozes off. I am also feeling very tired. It is terribly hot in the aging Chevrolet. The air conditioning is no match for the outside temperature of 129 °F. It is just my luck that this is the hottest day of the year so far in Iraq.

Abu Saeed is now in a deep sleep, as are his wife Aisha, their daughter Shahla and little Ali. I wish I could doze off too! All around us, desert, endless desert. It would be such a splendid landscape, if it were not for all the burned-out cars and reminders of the war.

I think back to my first two trips to Iraq in 2002 and 2003, a few weeks before the war began. I recall the beauty of the country and the boundless hospitality of the Iraqis I met back then, and also their anxious, even imploring looks when they asked me if I thought the imminent war could still be averted, and their silent resignation when I said the decision to go to war had probably long since been taken, whatever the outcome of the dispute over weapons of mass destruction.

I think of the children of Baghdad and Mosul, to whom our visit just before the invasion gave some glimmer of hope—hope that the war they were all talking about might prove to be just a bad dream. I think of all the Iraqis, to whom I promised to do everything in my power to lobby for a peaceful solution to the Iraq conflict—and of my helplessness, the helplessness of many journalists as they watched the American war machine lumbering down the wrong road, unable to impede it even for an instant with facts and arguments. How naive those efforts all were!

Zaid and the Old Man

Abu Saeed has woken up. This time he is the one to interrupt my train of thought. He wants to assure me once again that the Iraqi resistance categorically rejects violence against civilians. He turns to me and tells me about the plan in early 2007 to detonate a roadside bomb on Ishrin Street, one of the main streets in Ramadi, as a Humvee patrol passes by. Abu Saeed talks very quietly but with great intensity:

"One of my nephews, Zaid, was given the job of setting off the bomb. As the convoy approached, an old man sat down on a stone just opposite the spot where the bomb had been hidden. Zaid stared at him in dismay and waved to him from a distance to try to make him move. In just a few seconds he would have to trigger the detonation. Zaid started to shake and tears were trickling down his face. When the convoy was level with the bomb, he knew he had to set the bomb off at once.

"But he did not activate the bomb. White as a sheet, he slowly opened his fist, careful not to touch the activator. He let the convoy pass, unharmed.

"He went to his comrades and handed them the activator without saying a word. They all embraced him because he had spared the old man. They said they would have acted exactly the same way and that it was right not to detonate the bomb."

Abu Saeed turns away as he stops talking. "Can I meet Zaid?" I ask after a long silence. "You shall meet him," he says and falls silent again. But Zaid has caught my attention and I cannot get this young man out of my mind.

Abu Saeed's Story

After a while I ask Abu Saeed if he had lost any family members in the war. He bites his lip. Every family in Ramadi has lost somebody, he says. His eldest brother was detained two years ago on suspicion of being a resistance fighter. He has never returned, and his family now fears the worst.

Abu Saeed estimates that up to 40,000 Iraqis are locked away in American prisons. His eldest son, Saeed, who is 18, and his nephew Rashid were arrested in the winter of 2005 in Ramadi, also for allegedly fighting in the resistance. But neither of them was active in the resistance at the time.

First they were thrown into the American jail in Ramadi. They were beaten and kicked during their initial interrogations. To force a confession, they were not allowed any sleep for days on end. Saeed was released, but Rashid was transferred to Camp Bucca,[7] one of the British and later American prisons in Basra in the south of the country.

Rashid, a lanky, quiet boy, spent eight months in Camp Bucca. When he came home, he was almost unrecognizable—so agitated, sick and haggard. In Camp Bucca, Abu Saeed continues, Rashid had to share a small tent with several other prisoners. The tent did not protect them against the cold wind and sand storms in winter or the brutal heat of summer.

On one occasion, Rashid failed to act on a guard's order immediately, so they took away his mattress and curtailed his toilet breaks. A short while later he came down with a bad case of flu and had a high fever, but to punish him further, they did not let him see a doctor. He was beaten and kicked repeatedly. After Rashid came home, it took his parents weeks to build up his strength again.

The wounds on his body have healed, but those on his soul will stay with him forever. After his stay in Camp Bucca, Rashid immediately joined the resistance. Young people in the West would probably do the same, says Abu Saeed.

Up to 80,000 Iraqis are being held in Iraqi government prisons, often in overcrowded quarters. In Jaderiya prison, for example, at times 180 people were crammed into a space of 200 square meters (2,100 sq. ft.). They had to take it in turns to lie down and sleep because there was so little room. The sanitary conditions in the prisons are indescribable.

The American occupiers hand over resistance fighters they find particularly troublesome to the notorious Iraqi interior ministry, which mercilessly hounds opponents of the government. Those held by the ministry are almost always tortured, and many are killed. Their bodies turn up every few days in dozens, or even in hundreds, on the outskirts of Baghdad, in rubbish dumps or in the Tigris. They are so mutilated they have become unrecognizable. Abu Saeed says he fears that is what may have happened to his elder brother. The American occupiers turn a blind eye to these killings by the Iraqi authorities, because American law does not permit them to execute Iraqi prisoners themselves. At any rate, the United States has not undertaken any significant steps to stop such killings.

When I voice my doubts about his interpretation of events, Abu Saeed responds bitterly. In a hushed voice he tells me that in Iraq there are "well over a hundred American and Iraqi Guantánamos."* This is just one of the many hidden tragedies in his country. The Red Cross and human rights organizations have issued several detailed reports on these camps, but the Western media are evidently not interested. The prisoners in Iraq's Guantánamos are in a much worse state than those in the camp on Cuba. Among the thousands of people seized from their homes by the Americans, usually at night, there are many old or disabled people, and even children. Many are held in tents, like Rashid, or containers or even in latrines. Their life is hell, says Abu Saeed.

---

* Unnamed author: Turkey: Abu-Ghurayb torture victim tells reporters about his prison ordeal. *BBC Monitoring Europe*, supplied by BBC Worldwide Monitoring, NTV Television, Istanbul, Transcript, March 25, 2006: "[…] Haj Ali al-Qaysi, one of the victims in the photographs that disclosed the scandal in Abu Ghurayb prison and a person who has become the symbol of the torture in Iraq, has said that there are 300,000 prisoners in the U.S. prisons in Iraq. […] He said: 'The conditions in the prisons in Al-Fallujah and Al-Aqr are far worse than the ones in Abu Ghurayb. […] The U.S. Army has 26 prisons in the country […]. We do not have official figures on the number of people in the other 150 prisons. […] Our women are still being raped and our men are still being insulted. […] When I told them that the treatment of my hand was not finished, the U.S. soldiers crushed it with their boots and told me: This is a dose of U.S. aspirin. […] After so much torture, they simply said: It was a misunderstanding. […] the United States wants to trigger a civil war in that country. It will never succeed,' Qaysi stressed, 'because there is an all out resistance against the occupiers and the collaborators. There are no ethnic clashes.'"

See also in detail: Global Policy Forum and partners: Report: War and Occupation, 4: Detention and Prisons, January 2007, http://globalpolicy.org/security/issues/iraq/occupation/report/detention.htm

See also: Unnamed author: More Than 250 Iraqi Torture Victims come Forward to Sue CACI for Participating in Conspiracy to Torture, According to Legal Team. *PR Newswire*, December 18, 2007, www6.lexisnexis.com/publisher/EndUser? Action=UserDisplayFullDocument&orgId=574&topicId=100018896&docId=l:718080097&start=6

See also: Cole, Juan: Former US interrogator recounts torture cases in Afghanistan and Iraq. *Informed Comment*, December 10, 2007, www.juancole.com/2007/12/former-us-interrogator-recountstorture.html

Women are also often thrown in jail, he continues. The idea is that they are likely to inform on members of their family in order to be released. Many are raped in the American and the Iraqi prisons. Men are raped too. Sometimes, female prisoners are forced to watch men being raped. Abu Saeed says he can introduce me to people in Amman or Damascus who have witnessed such disgusting crimes.*

A well-known member of the Iraqi parliament recently states

---

* Unnamed author: Testimony from American jails in Iraq. The activity: women under occupation. *Arab Women Network, World Social Forum 2007*, Nairobi, January 2007: "I'm a young lady from Iraq [...]. My story starts in the night of 13/1/2004. [...] I heard screams and voices of planes and military vehicles [...] they opened the front door with bombs and entered. [...] they have taken us after putting our heads in black bags [...] they took me to the investigation room. [...] The nights were even harder as the soldiers get drunk and start turning the lights on and off, and they put water over us and leave their dogs to scare us, in this night they bring men from their rooms and raped them in front of our eyes as if saying see what's happening to your men! [...] They took me to the interrogation room and separated me from my mother, who was also kept along with me in the same prison. We were kept apart for twenty days then we were allowed to meet but without physical contact. My mother was told that if she does not confess, they would rape her daughter. I was led out of the interrogation room with a black hood over my head and I was made to hear a gun shot. I was told that my mother was shot; they played the same game with my mother. There is a report by Daini/Daayni, on the torture in U.S.-prisons."

See also the following report from the same young woman (excerpts): "The daughter of a well known Iraqi politician, her name is Zimam Istabrah, was with me in prison in a small cell, it was the airport prison. Music was kept at a loud level and water was regularly thrown into the cells. The Iraqi warden told me that the U.S. troops take drugs and drink alcohol. They forced me to watch the rape of one young Iraqi prisoner who was in the company of an elder man. In the room, where the rape took place there was a dining table and a computer table. The prisoner was thrown and kept down by his arms on one of these tables by an American soldier, while the other penetrated him from behind. The men were both stripped naked. The group was led by a soldier of Egyptian origin. I was pulled by my hair and forced to watch this scene. Zimam saw another case of rape. I was also threatened with rape. The Iraqi leadership was kept in the same prison. [...] I represent the Iraqi women's prisoner association; I myself was in prison, therefore I missed my final exams at the university. The suffering in U.S. prisons in Iraq is great." Manan, daughter of Abdul Rahim, born on January 13,1984.

that in 2006 there were 65 proven cases of rape committed against young women in American and Iraqi prisons.[8] The real number is probably much higher.

In Iraq's Guantánamos, Iraqis learn that in the eyes of the West they are worthless. Abu Saeed says he and many of his friends will never forget the words of the highest-ranking American jailer, General Geoffrey Miller who said Iraqi prisoners should be treated "like dogs" and never allowed to believe at any point that they are anything "more than a dog."[9]

Abu Saeed turns away and lovingly strokes the head of his little son. He clearly doesn't want to talk anymore. Perhaps he is right: What is the use of him talking and me writing about all this?

After a long pause I ask him again if any members of his family have been killed. Abu Saeed, this good-natured, friendly Iraqi businessman, becomes even more serious. He thinks long and hard whether to tell me, and what to tell me.

Then, without turning towards me, he says four of his relatives were shot and killed in 2003, shortly after the invasion, in a helicopter attack. They were going for a walk beside the Euphrates, which runs through Ramadi. The pilot probably suspected they wanted to bury bombs in the river bank. But all they were doing was going for an afternoon stroll.

Abu Saeed stares straight ahead. He clearly does not want me to see his stony expression. In April 2004, American aircraft dropped a bomb on the house of one of his nephews—in retaliation for an attack by resistance fighters. The nephew, his wife and their two small children were killed instantly.

In August 2005 his favorite uncle, Ahmad, was shot and killed in gunfire from a passing Humvee and his son seriously wounded. It took the U.S. troops twenty days to place Ahmed's body on the doorstep of his family's home. That same month, two other relatives were killed by American snipers as they were irrigating their fields.

Abu Saeed says he lives in Al-Jazeera, a very pretty part of Ramadi. During Ramadan, the month of fasting, in 2005, sixteen members of his extended family were in the mosque there for prayers one night. After prayers, the 16 men were chatting in the doorway, when suddenly an American plane bombed the mosque. The huge force of the explosion tore his relatives to pieces. They were killed instantly. Parts of their bodies were strewn across the road and the neighboring gardens, and were even hanging in the branches of the trees that surround the mosque.

Such reckless attacks on mosques by occupying forces are not unique to Ramadi. Once, after a bomb went off in Baghdad, an *imam* called for blood donors over the loudspeaker. The Americans responded by sending in helicopters to bomb the mosque and shooting the imam.

Abu Saeed has been so calm until now, but suddenly he starts to cry, and his whole body heaves as he sobs. Little Ali, who had been asleep, now looks at me reproachfully. He must think I said something nasty to his father. With his tiny hands, Ali tries to stroke his father's face. I am angry at myself tormenting Abu Saeed with my painful questions. And Abu Saeed seems to be angry at himself because he cannot hold back the tears.

Almost with an air of defiance, he continues after a while:

"The reason the Americans gave for the bombing raid was that the district where the mosque was located supported the resistance. But on that basis one could bomb all of Iraq to smithereens," says Abu Saeed. He takes several deep breaths. He does not want to show that he is still fighting back the tears. He again stares straight ahead.

Western politicians are strange heroes, he resumes. They protest in Moscow and Beijing against human rights abuses, but in Washington they remain silent. More than 50 members of his extended family have been killed, including several youngsters who had their whole lives ahead of them. He and his wife, Abu Saeed says, have long since stopped counting the dead. Do I still want to know why almost all Iraqis support the resistance? I shake my head.

Al-Jazeera, the Island

In the distance I see palm groves. Ramadi, surrounded by palm trees? That does not look the way I had imagined the former stronghold of Al-Qaeda in the war-torn Sunni triangle. Everyone in the car is awake now. Ali rubs his eyes and looks up to see if his father is all right again. Shahla looks a little grumpy as she stretches and then smoothes down her hair.

We cross the dark-blue Euphrates. Moussa has taken his foot off the accelerator and we coast towards the first checkpoint. A group of masked Iraqi police officers has installed a machine gun in the burned-out wreck of a car. One of them points his weapon at Moussa's window. When he sees my German passport, the whole palaver begins again.

The tension dissipates when the masked officer asks Abu Saeed how much he wants for me. Anbar province, of which Ramadi is the capital, is notorious for smuggling, highway robbery and kidnappings. Abu Saeed answers dryly, "You can't afford him."

With a shrug, Moussa closes his window.

We again negotiate a slalom course around concrete walls, gun emplacements, and barbed wire barriers. On our right is an imposing watchtower camouflaged with nets. Machine guns peep out of its window. It is the American headquarters in Ramadi, in one of Saddam Hussein's former palaces. After the fall of Baghdad, the Iraqi dictator first set up camp in Ramadi. "Put your camera down!" Abu Saeed hisses as I try to take photos of this sinister-looking building towering over all the others.

We turn down a dusty unpaved road lined with tall date palms to get to Al-Jazeera, a village-like oasis on the edge of Ramadi where Abu Saeed and his family live. The name means "island." In front of us, there are more roadblocks and masked policemen.

Moussa stops in a small alley. Abu Saeed whispers to me, "get out at once. The neighbors mustn't see you." I walk quickly through a large metal gate into a small garden. I see a single-story house built of rough gray stones stuck together with white cement. This is where Abu Saeed's family lives, together with the family of his younger brother Abu Hamid. The center of Ramadi is just a stone's throw away on the other side of the Euphrates.

The garden is full of cheerful, laughing children. In Iraq,

school is out for the summer from July until September. Two of the little ones have tied empty plastic water bottles under their arms. That means they want to go swimming in the river. But it takes more than two hours to get to the Euphrates because of all the barriers. It used to take just 10 minutes. They won't be taking a refreshing dip in the river today. But they can still dream of going swimming.

The older children are watching television with their parents in a baking hot reception room. A few days earlier Iraq's national soccer team had just won the Asian Cup for the first time ever.[10] The family watch in awe and disbelief as the goals are shown again and again on Iraqi television.

The Iraqi national squad is made up of Shi'ites and Sunnis, Arabs and Kurds. The decisive goal in the final against Saudi Arabia was shot by Younes Mahmoud, who is a Sunni, after a corner by Hawar, who is a Kurd. Midfield schemer Karrar Jassim is a Shi'ite. "If we stick together, we can achieve anything," says Abu Saeed, as he discreetly wipes away a tear. He is not the only member of his family whom I notice crying.

By now almost all the men, boys and girls have gathered in the reception room. It is a good opportunity for me to unpack the medical supplies I have brought from Germany as a gift for my hosts. My Iraqi friends from Baghdad, as well as Abu Saeed, had asked me to pretend to be a doctor as long as possible. Should there be any complicated cases, Abu Saeed promised he would call on a doctor he knows in Ramadi for assistance.

The children look impressed as I explain to Abu Saeed what the different medicines in my medicine chest are for. But when

I say they have to be kept cool/stored in a cool place, everybody starts to laugh.

There is electricity from the municipality for only a few hours each day. And the old generator in the house rarely runs for more than an hour without breaking down. And fuel has become so expensive in Iraq that the family could not afford to keep the generator running day and night. Before the American invasion, a liter of gas cost between one and two cents. Now it costs between 40 cents and a dollar. In some towns, Baquba for example, the price of one liter has reached two dollars.* Baquba is only 100 kilometers (62 miles) from Iraq's second biggest oil field.

It is 6 o'clock in the evening. It has become so hot indoors that everybody goes out into the garden. The huge palm trees cast long shadows. I go to the bathroom and take a shower. The sun has heated up the water in the metal tank so much that I almost burn myself. Still I have rarely enjoyed a shower so much. I go back into Abu Saeed's garden and feeling relaxed, sit down on one of the white plastic chairs.

The garden is made up of a lawn about 20 meters long and 15

---

* Baker-Hamilton Report (2006), p. 20: "The Iraqi government is not effectively providing its people with basic services: electricity, drinking water, sewage, health care, and education. In many sectors, production is below or hovers around pre-war levels. In Baghdad and other unstable areas, the situation is much worse. [...] One American official told us that Baghdad is run like a 'Shia dictatorship' because Sunnis boycotted provincial elections in 2005, and therefore are not represented in local government."

See also: Ali, Ahmed: Irak: Baquba kollabiert. Gewalt macht Alltagsleben zum russischen Roulette (Iraq: Baquba collapses. Forces turn everyday life into Russian roulette). *Islamische Zeitung*, August 1, 2007, www.islamische-zeitung.de/?id=9141

See also: Unnamed author: Minister goes in Iraq oil crisis. *BBC News*, December 30, 2005, http://news.bbc.co.uk/2/hi/middle_east/4569360.stm

meters wide (66 x 49 ft.), framed by narrow flowerbeds. The children find a football without much air in it and start to play with their bare feet. Five boys aged about 10 are pitted against three young men of about 20. The older team can hardly keep up with the young boys who compensate for their physical inferiority with all kinds of tricks.

Zaid and the "Double Stepover"

Abu Saeed's four-year old son Ali is watching rather forlornly from the sidelines. He wants to play too but he is too young. When the teams stop for a break—the temperature is after all still 113 °F—I take the ball and try to teach Ali a trick: the so-called "double stepover," something German national team midfielder Bastian Schweinsteiger performs to perfection.

I was taught the trick a few weeks earlier in the English Garden, a well-known public park in Munich, by my 16-year-old soccer buddy Enis, whose family comes from Turkey. At least in theory I know exactly how to do it: You make a circling movement with your right foot above the ball, out to the right, then the same thing with your left foot—and then you should pass the opponent.

Ali is fascinated as he watches me. He seems to think I am a great coach. My movements are so slow even a four-year-old can understand. The three older boys—all nephews of Abu Saeed—find it very amusing. One of them asks if he could also demonstrate the trick for Ali. He performs a double stepover about three times faster than I did. Ali looks at me with a quizzical expression. With the help of his father, I try to explain that that was the fast version. Then the boys resume their match. Ali and I watch. He thinks I am OK, perhaps because he can't do the trick any faster than I can.

One of Abu Saeed's nephews plays brilliantly—the one who performed the "double Schweinsteiger" at triple speed. I ask Abu Saeed who this tall and smart boy is. Abu Saeed answers with a benign smile. "That is Zaid."

Zaid? Zaid, the resistance fighter? I catch my breath for a moment. So this is the young man who could not bring himself to detonate a roadside bomb because an old man was nearby. I am astounded. I never thought an Iraqi resistance fighter would look like that.

At the end of the soccer game there is a penalty shootout— from about half the usual distance. The goal is an old metal bed. Zaid is goalkeeper. Half the balls go astray, Zaid keeps the rest out of his goal with his great reflexes. After each player has had his turn, Zaid calls over to me and says I should try too.

I am very bad at penalty shots. I am also still wearing my ankle-length dishdasha and really do not want to make a fool of myself. But they all want me to have a go, so I put on a brave face. I position the ball, step back two meters and then launch my attack—no doubt an odd sight in my nightgown-like robe. As I kick the ball, I feel the dishdasha rip up to the level of my knee and think to myself I should never have got into this.

But then I notice that the ball is in the goal, right beside the left-hand bedpost. The young boys cheer and laugh and tease the older ones. Zaid is incredulous. He pulls the ball out from between the bedsprings. He wants revenge and challenges me to shoot again. But I decline. One should not push one's luck.

In the meantime, two young boys are directing a flock of bleating sheep into their enclosure on the property next door. The muezzin is calling the faithful to evening prayers. The men—Abu Saeed, Abu Hamid and their nephews, including Zaid—fetch nomad rugs from the house and start to pray together. Abu Saeed leads the prayers. Little Ali stands reverentially next to his father and tries to imitate his every move.

Behind the house the women are cooking two chickens in a homemade wood-fired clay oven. They plucked the birds' feathers during the soccer match. They can't use the much more modern gas oven standing nearby. A 60 cm (24 in.) canister of gas used to cost 12 cents under Saddam Hussein and now costs 20 dollars. Like most people in Ramadi, Abu Saeed cannot afford that. A country with such an abundance of oil cannot provide its own people with fuel.

The women call the homemade clay oven their "Bush oven." One of the women laughs and calls out sarcastically "Thank you, Mr. Bush! We always wanted to know how people cooked in the Middle Ages." Despite the difficult conditions, the women succeed in preparing a delicious soup, two tender chickens, okra and curry, which they place on a tablecloth spread out on the lawn.

As is customary in Iraq, the men and women eat separately. The women are sitting about 10 meters (33 ft.) away and appear to be having lots of fun. They seem to be talking about us, as they keep looking in our direction, giggling and whispering.

Two of the four adult women are wearing the *abaya*, a typical Iraqi black robe that covers the entire body. Two others are wearing bright patterned ankle-length dresses. They all have their hair covered with a *hijab*, the traditional headscarf.

The young girls are all wearing European-style clothes. And this evening they have put on their finest. Shahla is sporting a trendy jeans skirt and pink T-shirt, her little cousins colorful dungarees or tailored dresses. They have pinned up their hair and tied it with bright ribbons.

After the meal, we drink strong sweet tea in small glasses. The sun is setting. We hear children playing nearby. It seems so peaceful—were it not just three kilometers to one of the biggest U.S. military bases in Iraq, a daily and very visible reminder to the Iraqis that their country is under occupation. Only in Baghdad does the United States have more troops stationed than here in the desert province of Anbar.

Suddenly Apache military helicopters appear and circle above us for several minutes at a height of 50 meters (164 ft.). Abu Saeed looks up sullenly. Above the helicopters we see an American reconnaissance plane, reportedly an F-16, on its routine evening patrol over the so-called "Sunni Triangle." Suddenly the sense of peace evaporates. The conversations break off; the women withdraw into the house.

Zaid is sitting opposite me, silently. He is a good-looking boy. He probably knows that, because when he talks to his female cousins, he deploys his charm strategically. But I sense that he is trying to hide something. Whenever he thinks nobody is watching, his eyes look sad and thoughtful. His sunny-boy laugh is that of a young man desperately trying not to lose his mind in this mad war.

I very much want to hear his story. But Zaid does not want to talk. He does not want to endanger his family; he does not want to be sent to Guantánamo on Cuba or to one of the Guantánamos in Iraq. Nor does he want to tell me about what he and his family have gone through. I try for half an hour to persuade him, but I see that he cannot and will not talk.

Abu Saeed, who is listening to our dialog silently, puts his arm around Zaid's shoulder and says to me: "Give him time. He has to think it over. Perhaps tomorrow he will tell you his story. He has to talk to his father first; it is not only about Zaid. And in any case you are going to get to know many other resistance fighters, just like you wanted to."

"I understand, but I don't want a story that has been specially selected for me," I reply. "I want Zaid's story." Abu Saeed smiles. "Be patient. You shall hear his story, Insha'allah."

Zaid wants to go home, and we accompany him to the front gate. Abu Saeed then resumes his favorite activity, talking on the phone. He makes a number of calls on his big old mobile phone. He evidently talks to Zaid's father, because he mentions Zaid's name several times.

First Night in Ramadi

It is pitch black now, and the imam of Al-Jazeera has joined us, a corpulent man with cropped white hair. He lectures me on how much the three monotheist religions have in common and explains that for him as a Muslim, Moses and Jesus are among the greatest of prophets.

I am no longer feeling very receptive, and ask him if he has read the Bible. He says he hasn't but can recite the Qur'an from memory, all 114 suras. I congratulate him, and in a dignified manner he stands up in order to proceed to night prayers. The seven men in their white robes bowing in the direction of Mecca are an impressive sight. The imam of Al-Jazeera leads the prayers. The skill with which this bulky man conducts the quite strenuous prayer movements is impressive.

Little Ali, standing with the garden hose in his hand in front of the group of praying men, is impressed. So much so, that he drops the hose, and unintentionally sprays the imam with water from head to toe. But the imam continues to pray without missing a beat or showing any surprise. The women and girls, however, who had come back out into the garden after the helicopters had left and were sitting nearby on the lawn, can hardly suppress their laughter.

Ali is getting bored as the prayers go on and on. He fetches the airless football and asks me, by imitating the way I had moved my feet, to show him the double stepover again, in front of the group of praying men.

The women can no longer contain themselves and burst out laughing. I put my finger to my lips, to signal to Ali that I can't show him soccer tricks now while his family are praying and the women are all laughing.

About two hours later, shortly before midnight, Abu Saeed

points out the flares being shot into the night sky about two kilometers away. They bathe parts of Ramadi in brilliant light. Helicopters are in the skies looking for targets or people. The nightly reconnaissance mission lasts 20 minutes. No shots are fired. Eventually the sinister firework display comes to an end.

I ask Abu Saeed where I am to sleep. He laughs cheerfully: "Wherever you like." In the "well-heated" reception room or, like the family, outside on the lawn, where it is a "cool 95 °F." The grid has been down for hours, and the generator has already broken down again.

I trudge into the reception room, but it is so hot there that after 10 minutes I am drenched in sweat. Resignedly, I return to the garden. A row of plastic chairs and cardboard boxes draped with mats separate the men from the women. At some distance from both groups, I lie down on a thin foam mattress under a large date palm.

The last time I slept out of doors was in the '80s with the Mujahideen in the Hindu Kush. I decided then to avoid doing so again. For me, this is a very exhausting way to spend the night. But what the hell, I don't have any choice.

The sky is clear and full of stars. I can't get to sleep, and stare into the sky, asking myself what on earth made me come here. I would so like to be at home sleeping in my comfortable, cozy bed. As it is, I am lying wide-awake in my sweaty dishdasha under a date palm.

Suddenly, at about 2 a.m., just as I am about to fall asleep, I hear the sound of helicopters again and gunfire. I jump up and go over to the garden wall. A gun battle is underway at the spot where the flares had been fired a few hours earlier. Helicopters hover over the area. I hear explosions. It all lasts half an hour, and then it is over.

Abu Saeed has come over and is now quietly standing beside me. I ask him how come there is fighting if there is a ceasefire in Ramadi. Abu Saeed smiles and says he doesn't know. The resistance is made up of many groups and they are hard to control. And perhaps there are still some scattered foreign Al-Qaeda fighters here, he says.

And in any case, the ceasefire only applies to Ramadi itself, and the city has a diameter of just a few kilometers. All around the city fighting continues, especially at night. Many members of the tribes that cooperate with the Americans during the day fight them at night. You can hire an Iraqi, but you cannot buy him.

But there are battles during the day as well. This afternoon a Humvee was blown up not far from Ramadi, on the road to Baghdad. Several U.S. soldiers were killed, but also some resistance fighters. It is only in the center of Ramadi that there is no fighting—at least most of the time, says Abu Saeed.

As quietly as he had come over to talk to me, he goes back to his bivouac. And I lie down on my thin mattress and, at last, fall into a deep and dreamless sleep.

Zaid's Dreams

A little after six in the morning, two American Apache helicopters wake me as they thunder over the house. It is light already. The children are all bundled up in blankets on their foam mattresses. Abu Hamid shoos them out of their beds. At six o'clock, it is time to get up in Ramadi.

I try to ignore the commotion; I just want to carry on sleeping peacefully. But I don't stand a chance. Two helicopters fly low over the house. What a merciless wake-up service! I stumble sleepily to the communal shower. I stand for several minutes under the stream of water, which is still warm.

Abu Saeed sees how tired I still am and brings me a large mug of black coffee. Slowly, my spirits rise. He also brings me home-made pita and jam. I munch away appreciatively. Then I try to shave looking into a clouded mirror without destroying my moustache. I am glad the mirror only yields a vague impression of my face. Few people look good after long journeys and short nights.

I find a shady corner of the garden and start to write some notes. Suddenly somebody taps me on the shoulder from behind. I turn round and find myself looking at Zaid's face. "You wanted to talk to me," he says quietly and a little shyly.

Zaid is wearing blue jeans, a washed-out red T-shirt and fake Adidas sneakers. In his left hand he is holding and hiding, rather like a schoolboy, a packet of Gauloises cigarettes made in Syria. When Al-Qaeda were on the rampage in Ramadi, smoking was prohibited and even dangerous.

Zaid set off at six o'clock from his home in the Al-Sufia neighborhood. Getting to Al-Jazeera used to take 15 minutes, now it takes two and a half hours, because of all the roadblocks and checkpoints. Zaid has talked to his father. And the father has given him permission to tell me his story. Slowly and quietly,

Zaid begins to do just that.

He was born in 1986 during the Iraq-Iran war. His father Mohammed and his mother Amira own a small grocery store in Al-Sufia. They managed to get by under very difficult conditions during the war and then during the regime of the sanctions imposed on Iraq. They always had food, even if it was sometimes only bread.

Times got much harder after the Gulf War following Iraq's invasion of Kuwait. Iraq lost the war in 1991 to a multinational force led by the United States. The economic sanctions made life very difficult. Zaid's parents could rarely afford vegetables or meat for their family of seven.

Zaid recalls that his parents suffered much more than their three sons and two daughters. Whenever they found something good to eat, they gave it to their children. They had to work twice as hard to meet their family's needs. Zaid says a number of young children in the neighborhood died of malnutrition and poor medical care, because the health service in Iraq collapsed as a result of the sanctions imposed by the United Nations Security Council.

He has few positive memories of this period. He and his friends spent all their free time playing soccer on a makeshift pitch. Barefoot, of course. He often came home with bleeding toes.

Whenever his father got angry, because Zaid had once again not done his homework, he hid behind his mother. She always protected him. And whenever he got into trouble at school for his pranks—which Zaid recounts with merriment—his mother always stood up for him against his strict father, no matter what he had done. And he did plenty.

Once his class had an English exam. He had written some English words on his notebook, which was lying on the desk beside him. Apparently the words had nothing to do with the test, but his teacher was convinced Zaid was trying to cheat and sent him out of the room despite him protesting heavily.

Zaid was very angry, but above all bored, hanging around alone in the schoolyard. Then he had what he considered a brilliant idea. He went back into the classroom and told the teacher he was not the only one who had cheated, seven of his friends had also done so. And he pointed to the seven best soccer players in the class, with whom he used to play after school.

The seven were furious as they were sent out, and threatened to beat Zaid up. But he said he had only named them so that they could go and play some soccer. He had been so bored without them. His friends laughed, and they made peace. While the others were sweating over the English test inside, Zaid and his friends went off to enjoy a game of soccer.

Another time, at the end-of-year party, Zaid presented the math instructor with a can of Pepsi on behalf of the class, because they had chosen him as their favorite teacher. Flattered, he accepted the honor and the cool drink.

He had not noticed that Zaid had shaken the can vigorously. The teacher pulled the tab and was promptly sprayed by the sticky brown liquid all over his face and suit.

The kids were delighted, the teacher less so. Of course, trouble was waiting at home. But as always, his mother shielded Zaid from his furious father.

His mother is a great cook, Zaid tells me. Whenever there

was trouble, she would make one of his favorite dishes—kebabs, or dolma, stuffed tomatoes or stuffed paprika. Zaid smiles happily when he talks about his mother.

On September 11, 2001, when Al-Qaeda terrorists fly two airplanes into the World Trade Center, Zaid is a boy of 15. A few weeks later, the first speculation over a connection between Iraq and Al-Qaeda are aired on television. There are discussions about the possibility of the United States waging war not only against Afghanistan, but also against Iraq.

Zaid thinks that is rubbish. He does not know anybody in his small world who even knows what Al-Qaeda is.

He thinks it is absurd propaganda by the United States to claim that Iraq has weapons of mass destruction, given the economic sanctions and years of United Nations inspections. How could Iraq have produced weapons of mass destruction? In 2001 it was "the most closely observed country in the world," Zaid says. How could one believe anything so stupid? Even in the West no one really believes that. People can't be that stupid or malicious. That could never be a reason to go to war! There must be some justice in the world, even for Iraq.

When the war does indeed start, in March 2003, Zaid is sure Iraq will win. He believes Saddam Hussein, who has often said the United States doesn't stand a chance against Iraq. Zaid attends the daily prayers at which the people of Ramadi ask for God's help in these days of hardship. He sits with his friends in front of the television for hour upon hour, watching the news about the war.

When a big sandstorm halts the Americans' advance for a few days, Zaid thinks the tide has turned. At least God is on the side of the Iraqis. And when the information minister, Mohammad Said al-Sahhaf*, says Bush, Blair and Rumsfeld were a "funny trio" and "God would roast their stomachs in hell at the hands of Iraqis," Zaid believes every word.

Even with American tanks in the center of Baghdad, Al-Sahhaf still declares grandly, before the world's journalists, "I give you a threefold guarantee, there are no American soldiers in Baghdad; ... they are retreating on all fronts; ... their soldiers are committing suicide by the hundreds on the gates of Baghdad." Zaid says now he knows that people in the West screamed with laughter listening to Al-Sahhaf, but in Iraq people were clinging desperately to his words; what he said was their last hope. But eventually defeat could not be concealed any longer, and for Zaid, who was now 17, the world fell apart.

American tanks first appear in Ramadi at the end of April 2003. They are met with a hail of sandals, stones and vegetables. Nobody is afraid of them, but nobody cheers or welcomes the Americans either.

The occupation of Ramadi proceeded in stages: U.S. troops first secured the major crossroads, then the most important buildings, then they closed some roads, and finally they divided the city into various zones cut off from each other.

The Iraqi troops simply went home, Zaid continues, and hid their uniforms. All the members of the armed forces and security services were dismissed by the Americans and became unem-

---

* Mohammed Said al-Sahhaf was Saddam Hussein's Foreign Minister and later Information Minister of Iraq during the U.S. invasion. He was mockingly nicknamed "Baghdad Bob" by commentators in the U.S.

ployed overnight. Many joined the resistance, bringing with them their experience and their weapons. Others fled the country.

Life for the people of Ramadi became harder by the day. American planes bombed alleged pockets of resistance and killed entire families in the process. American snipers posted on roofs across the city shot at anything they thought was suspicious. They usually hit innocent people. Most resistance fighters know how to elude snipers, Zaid tells me.

In June 2004, Zaid gets his high school diploma, with pretty good grades. He is now 18. His plan is to study history at Ramadi's Anbar University, like his uncle Abu Saeed did, starting in the fall and then to become a teacher. Zaid knows all the tricks mischievous youngsters get up to, because he used to be one himself. His students won't be able to fool him; he wants to educate young people to become capable, confident citizens and show them that life is worth living. He is really looking forward to his future career.

That is why he has not taken an active role in the resistance, Zaid says. He is not really interested in military matters, but in history. And he did not want to endanger his family. His two brothers Haroun and Karim felt the same way. There is no military tradition in their family.

And then in June 2006, fate catches up with his small family. Zaid runs his left hand over his eyes to conceal his emotions. With his right hand, he helplessly begins to hit the grass.

Abu Saeed, who has joined us silently, puts his arm around Zaid's shoulders. "We have to go," he says, "The doctor has an appointment. You can carry on tomorrow." It is one in the afternoon, and at 118 °F it is a little cooler than the day before. We walk slowly to our Chevrolet, which is by now covered by dust. Zaid comes with us.

We drive along bumpy streets through the city of palms, past countless checkpoints, towards Al-Sufia. We go past Zaid's house, drive around one block twice, then suddenly turn back the way we had come, as if Moussa, our driver, wants to shake off somebody who was tailing us. That is probably what he is in fact doing.

Then we stop in front of a dilapidated house. A gate opens. We turn quickly into the courtyard. Abu Saeed carefully closes the gate. A group of five men are sitting next to the house; they look at us with interest as we vanish indoors.

We are in a sparsely furnished room with three old chairs and a low wooden table. It is so gloomy that I find it hard to adjust my vision. Abu Saeed says he had promised to introduce me to active resistance fighters. He is a man of his word. The men outside are fighters from various resistance groups, and they are willing to tell me their stories. But I should not ask their names or take any photographs. Apart from that, I can ask whatever I want.

I am astonished. It was so hard to get Zaid to talk—and here Abu Saeed has drummed up a whole bunch of resistance fighters! I accept his conditions. Abu Saeed goes to the door and gestures to the men. He sits down next to me as he is going to be my interpreter.

Omar

The first to join us at the wobbly table is Omar, a friendly, brawny 36-year-old Iraqi from Mosul. His handshake is so painfully firm

I vow just to say goodbye when he leaves. Omar is wearing a blue striped T-shirt and jeans. He looks like a young Bud Spencer, the star of many Spaghetti Westerns, except Omar looks much friendlier.

Omar has been fighting in the Iraqi resistance since the very beginning. He lost 10 members of his family, including his oldest son Mazin, when the American troops invaded. Mazin was nine years old when American soldiers shot him, Omar tells me.

He will never forget the look on the face of his dying son; his eyes were pleading: "Papa, help me. You always help me." But Omar could not help this time, and Mazin bled to death in his arms. Even some of the American soldiers were devastated as they watched Mazin die.

Omar's expression, so open and friendly a moment ago, is transformed. He lowers his head and tries to maintain his composure. After a while he says I should not ask him any more about his son. The memories are too painful.

When Omar joined the resistance, he received "comprehensive training" from former Iraqi Army officers. Now he leads a group of 250 resistance fighters based in Kirkuk and Tikrit.

His father and one of his brothers have been in prison for on and a half years, he says. But he does not know where. Families are rarely told. The Americans also detained him, Omar tells me. But after three months and 10 days he managed to escape.

In prison—he won't tell me which one—he was treated well by the American soldiers, even though he told them during interrogation that he was a resistance fighter. He was not tortured, and a doctor even treated his toothache. He was lucky, Omar says, in the midst of such misfortune.

He respects the soldiers who interrogated him, because they were humane, Omar says, even though he knows how bad things are in most prison camps. But he will never accept the Americans as occupiers of his country. Some of the American troops had even admitted that they were against the occupation of Iraq. They know they have no right to be here, says Omar.

His family lives on a farm, but Omar has not been to see them for a long time, because there are informers around, who cooperate with the occupiers. His mother died a year ago, but he could not attend her funeral, because he would have been arrested at once. They did not let his father attend his wife's funeral.

Omar is a devout Muslim and a Ba'athist nationalist, he says. After the chaos and the bloodshed caused by the invasion, the popularity of the Ba'athists increased. In particular, the way Saddam Hussein behaved at his execution gave the Ba'athists a boost.

Omar says he is proud that Saddam Hussein met his death with such dignity. Bush made a hero of Saddam.

I stand up to say goodbye to Omar. He looks at me thoughtfully and says very earnestly that the resistance never attacks journalists. I tell him that I am not a journalist but a media executive. He laughs and says that doesn't make any difference. He still considers me a guest in his country. Though, he adds, he is disappointed by the coverage of Iraq in the Western media.

He is astonished that no distinction is drawn between the Iraqi resistance to the occupation and the terrorism brought in from abroad that is directed against the civilian population.

He also finds it strange that the resistance is criticized for hiding in residential neighborhoods among civilians. Where should they be? The resistance doesn't have any barracks. Resistance fighters are freedom fighters. During the day, many have to go to work. Moreover, in most places the people all support the resistance.

Omar gets up and grasps my hand again with his vice-like enormous right hand, despite my vow not to make the same mistake again. Omar sees me grimacing with pain and shaking my right hand. He laughs and apologizes, saying next time he will just give me a hug. He adds that he hopes my country will never suffer as much misfortune as his; then he turns and strides out to the garden, to rejoin his comrades-in-arms.

Mohammed

My hand still hurts, as another man enters the room. He is of medium height and looks fatherly and elderly. In fact he is 42 years old and therefore 25 years younger than me. He is wearing a pair of gray pressed trousers and a short-sleeved brown shirt. He looks very dignified.

He introduces himself as Mohammed—which is probably not his real name. None of the men at this meeting wants to tell me his name, for security reasons. I look at his large hand and decide not to shake it. I put my right hand to my heart and bow—a greeting that has been customary in the Arab world for centuries.

Mohammed used to be a professor at Baghdad University. He is a Shi'ite. As a member of the Ba'athist party he joined the resistance a few weeks after the American invasion.

Now he heads a "united resistance group" made up of nationalists, Ba'athists and moderate Islamists. He is evidently/It is obvious that he is a leading figure in the Iraqi resistance. He is not only very erudite, but also astoundingly well informed about politics.

He tells me that he joined the resistance "in order to end the humiliation of the Iraqi people." During their nightly raids, the occupiers so often attack families in their homes and humiliate them. They regularly take away all the men, and sometimes even the women, old people and children, and lock them up in camps for months for no apparent reason.

Recently in Mosul, they arrested a frail man of over 70 because his son was said to belong to the resistance. The soldiers tied him up and left him lying on the stone floor for five days. Sitting comfortably in an armchair, they would take it in turns to rest their boots on his neck or face for hours to make him reveal where his son was. But the old man did not say a word.

And Mohammed's own brother, who is 50 and has a serious heart condition, was held without any medical care for weeks in a tiny cell in order to force him to reveal Mohammed's whereabouts.

Although he has never been to America, Mohammed considers the United States to be a great country. He is fighting U.S. troops because they are occupiers, not because they are Americans. He simply cannot fathom the stupidity of this war and of American politics. The U.S. Army doesn't stand a chance in Iraq. The resistance has long since attained military parity, if not more, and one day they will force the United States to pull out its forces.

Mohammed estimates that there are more than 100,000 active fighters in the resistance, and between 40 and 50 percent of them are independent nationalists or Ba'athists. The moderate Islamists

make up the other half. Most of the leaders are Ba'athists and former army officers, because they have the most military experience.

Less than five percent of the insurgents nationwide belong to
Al-Qaeda. Most of the leadership and the hard core of their fighters are foreigners. They have the most money. Al-Qaeda can even
afford to buy photographs and videos of attacks on the occupiers
from Iraqi resistance groups, and then claim its own fighters carried out those operations.

The extremists of Al-Qaeda are no freedom fighters. They are
pursuing other goals. They are not interested in bringing peace to
Iraq; they want the war with the Americans to continue for as long
as possible—and not only in Iraq. What is more, Al-Qaeda only
fights for the Sunnis, and that is not the Iraqi way: The multi-
confessional Iraqi resistance fights for everybody.

Just as bad as Al-Qaeda are the militias run by radical Shi'ite
politicians—especially the death squads of the Shi'ite Mahdi
Army. Many of these militias are funded by Iran. But the militias
loyal to some Sunni politicians are also abhorrent, Mohammed
tells me. And the private security contractors financed by the
United States are no better.[11] These "outsourced" parts of the
American armed forces are comprised of more than 100,000
highly paid people, and have enjoyed immunity ever since the invasion in 2003 thanks to a decree by Paul Bremer, who was then
head of the American-run civil administration.

The Blackwater Army in particular, the best-known American
private mercenary army in Iraq, is notorious for its ruthlessness
and brutality. The so-called "security" contractors employ not
only U.S. mercenaries but also ones from Latin America, Africa

and Asia to fulfill a variety of functions. They are responsible for protecting politicians and diplomats, for securing important deliveries in exchange for large sums of money, or guarding strategically important buildings and prisons. In Fallujah they have even taken part in military action.

Sometimes American intelligence agencies use the private security contractors for special operations. The hired helpers do the dirty work, things with which U.S. officials do not want to be associated. If a mercenary is injured or killed, there is no public announcement. That is all set out in their contracts.

Al-Qaeda, the Mahdi Army and the intelligence agencies of certain foreign powers are responsible for the abhorrent attacks on markets and mosques. Their aim is to discredit the Iraqi resistance, both at home and internationally, and to undermine the resolve and cohesion of the Iraqi people. The legitimate Iraqi resistance has nothing to do with such disgusting terrorism. True Iraqis do not kill innocent civilians.

One major cause of the current political problems within Iraq, says Mohammed, is that after the invasion, the United States distributed power on the basis of religious denomination. They thereby intentionally created the conflict between Sunnis and Shi'ites, which had never existed in this form, in order to divide the country.

It is as though after the Second World War, government positions and seats in parliament in Germany had been distributed on the basis of membership in the Catholic and Protestant churches.

At first, here in Iraq, people were hired even for ordinary jobs not because of their qualifications but their religious denomination or ethnic background. That was a source of great tension.

It was ultimately the same old strategy of "divide and rule" that the United States used throughout the Arab world to impede pan-Arabic nationalism. The United States made a conscious decision to ignore the fact that Iraq had already coalesced into a nation, with special features in the Kurdish north. Multi-ethnic and multi-confessional centers had long since emerged in Baghdad, Mosul and Basra.

Shi'ites and Sunnis lived together in harmony for centuries, Mohammed continues. The differences between the two branches of Islam are less important than those between Catholicism and Protestantism. In villages with only one mosque, for example, Sunnis and Shi'ites usually prayed together. What they have in common will soon become evident again, once the Americans withdraw.

To claim that a horrible civil war will erupt in Iraq if the United States pulls its troops out is an old trick. In 1920, British Prime Minister David Lloyd George also warned of a civil war if Britain withdrew its army. In response to that, the Iraqi tribes joined forces and rose up against the British colonial rulers.

Mohammed is very much the professor as he lectures me. The language of the conquerors is always the same: When the British marched into Baghdad in 1917, they announced they had not come as conquerors or enemies, but as liberators—rather like the United States in 2003. But they stayed for four decades. It is always the same story.

The Iraqi resistance conducts more than 1,000 military operations each week, currently about 180 per day.[12] These figures were confirmed by the Baker-Hamilton Report, which was written by senior U.S. experts. The nationalist and Ba'athist resistance is responsible for about 50 percent of these operations.

The resistance has weapons from the old Iraqi Army but also gratefully accepted modern American weapons, which the United States handed out generously and without much supervision after the invasion, and, of course, Iranian weapons. But they have to be bought at high prices on the black market, unlike the American weapons, most of which were free.

The Western media pay hardly any attention to the resistance's military activities. What is even worse, however, is that they almost completely ignore the 100–200 daily acts of violence, the bombings and the raids committed by the U.S. troops. As a rule they only report the one, two or three suicide bombings that occur each day, which are usually perpetrated by foreigners, and then claim they exemplify the violence that prevails within Iraq. The media thus play along with American war propaganda, whether intentionally or not.

"You only show on television terrorist suicide attacks organized from abroad, you never show the terrorism of the occupiers," Mohammed says quietly. All Arabic-language broadcasters that report fairly on the brutality of the U.S. Army and on the successes of the Iraqi resistance to the U.S. occupation come under massive pressure from the United States. The satellite television station Al Zawraa, for example, has been closed down in Cairo and in Baghdad because of its critical reporting on the United States.

Since the first battle for Fallujah, most resistance groups have CDs with satellite photographs of Iraq's major highways and important buildings, which are very useful for planning their attacks, even if they are not always up-to-date. In the digital age, laptop computers and Google Earth are part of a freedom fighter's equipment.

The resistance is not fighting to establish an Islamic theocratic state—unlike both Al-Qaeda, which is financed by Saudi "charitable organizations," and the radical Shi'ite militias, which are mostly funded by Iran. The resistance wants to install a secular constitution, Mohammed tells me. It wants to create a democratic state, in which all Iraqis feel represented, a state that is nationalist in orientation and, if the Ba'athists have their way, pan-Arabic as well. It will, of course, have its spiritual and intellectual roots in Islam.

Mohammed has the air of a benign scholar. It is hard to imagine him conducting military operations, deciding where to position a roadside bomb, or leading his men into battle. I have the impression that he would rather be back with his students at Baghdad University than take part in this dirty war, with all its boundless human tragedies.

For Mohammed, terrorists are people who kill civilians for political reasons. He therefore considers Al-Qaeda, the death squads run by certain politicians, and the U.S. government all to be terrorists. The soldiers of the U.S. government have demonstrably killed hundreds of thousands of civilians in Iraq, more than Al-Qaeda and all the militias together. "It is against this terrorism that we are fighting," says Mohammed, who then adds that it is a strange phenomenon that the Bush administration that is responsible for the murder of civilians every day, calls the Iraqi resistance a terrorist organization, even though it does not kill civilians.

Mohammed makes clear that he is not calling the young American soldiers in Iraq terrorists. They too are victims of this war—even though as a resistance leader he has a duty to fight them. The U.S. president is robbing not only the young of Iraq of their youth, but the young American soldiers as well. Almost 4,000 American soldiers have been killed and more than 30,000 have been severely wounded; but in the United States few talk about the wounded American soldiers, let alone the wounded Iraqis.

Mohammed has spoken with great seriousness. He is the kind of man one would like to hug when saying goodbye, in times of peace, that is—even if one does not share all his opinions. But Iraq is at war. So we bow and wish other well, "Salam alaikum—peace be with you!"

Ahmad

The heat in the room has become almost unbearable. But suddenly the power returns, and with a groan the air conditioning starts up again and slowly cools the air. Still, it is at least 104 °F in here.

I am looking at my notes and trying to put my thoughts in order when the next man I am to talk to enters. Standing in front of me, he asks almost shyly if he may take a seat. His name is Ahmad and he is from Ramadi. He is tall and thin. He sports a carefully trimmed goatee beard, and is wearing a gray kaftan. He is 30 years old, single, and used to be a construction worker.

Ahmad too wipes the sweat from his brow. While I drink water, he stills his thirst with hot sweet tea. Ahmad is very pale, unusually shy, and not very talkative. He tells his story haltingly and in a quiet voice.

At about noon on a sunny day in the fall of 2006, he was strolling in the almost deserted streets of Ramadi. He was on his way to do some shopping. He was walking slowly because it was very hot. He had a day off work and was in no rush. As he turned into Ishrin Street in the center of town, he did not notice how the American marksmen lying on the roofs of the buildings focussed their guns on him. He does not know why they shot at him. He had nothing to do with the resistance. He was just thankful for every day he stayed out of trouble and continued to have work. He did not earn much, but he could still help his family to get by.

The marksmen aimed at his crotch and fired; they destroyed his testicles and severely damaged his penis. The doctors in Ramadi patched him up as best they could, but there was not much they could save. He spent weeks in the hospital and is still receiving treatment, because the wounds are not healing.

Ahmad say he knew there were American sharpshooters in Ramadi but did not think they would shoot at ordinary people walking down the street. You never know in advance where the marksmen will take up position. It is a matter of chance. Sometimes they burst into homes and take children hostage. They lock the rest of the family into a room, so they cannot tell anyone what is taking place.

Ahmad still does not know what military aim these marksmen serve. It is rumored that they bet on who hits the most bull's-eyes in any one day. Since they shot him, he has supported the resistance as best he can.

Ahmad has shown no emotion during our conversation, and spoken very quietly. Then he stops talking. He had told me enough. He gets up shyly and says goodbye. He goes back to the other resistance fighters, who are still sitting in the garden.

Yussuf

The air conditioning has broken down again. The sweating can resume. I very much need a break; my mental faculties are waning, despite the huge amounts of water I have been drinking. As I am about to tell Abu Saeed, Yussuf suddenly appears in front of me. He is wearing a white dishdasha and a traditional white Arab headdress, held in place with a thick black cord.

At last, an Arab resistance fighter who looks just like the Western stereotype of an Arab Muslim! But to my great surprise, I am proven wrong: Yussuf is not a Muslim but a Christian resistance fighter. He is 35 years old, big, and tall.

He is almost always smiling as we talk. I ask why he seems to be in such a good mood. It is because he is a trader, he tells me, it is a good idea/habit to smile in a friendly manner. His slender fingers are playing with a string of black beads; it is not a rosary, but a *subhah*, Arab prayer beads.

Yussuf is just one of many Christian resistance fighters in Iraq.*

* For example: Unnamed author: Christians may take up arms. *News24.com*, December 9, 2004, www.news24.com/News24/World/Iraq/0,,2-10-1460_1631298,00.html: "More than 1,500 members of an Iraqi Christian group have gone to northern Iraq to try to protect Christians following attacks on churches in Baghdad and Mosul, the leader of the group said [...]. In an interview, Yonadem Kana, the leader of the Assyrian Democratic Movement in Iraq and a member of the Iraqi National Council, said the fighters have been deployed in Bakhdida near the northern city of

He comes from the Al-Dourah neighborhood of south Baghdad. More than 100,000 Christians used to live there together with 250,000 Muslims. More than half the Christians fled to escape the Christian invaders, the Sunni Al-Quaeda and the Shi'ite militias. Most went to Syria, which is well known for its friendliness towards Christians. Of the Christians who stayed, most support the resistance, Yussuf tells me with a smile.

He has never been a member of the Ba'ath party. He is not interested in politics. And he never liked Saddam Hussein. But he could not just stand by and watch his country be destroyed by foreign troops. The Americans killed three of his cousins, also Christians.

One day, American soldiers stormed his house at four o'clock in the morning, kicked in all the doors, shot at his car, which then went up in flames, and arrested his nephews and threw them in jail.

The Christians he knows see themselves above all as Iraqis, Yussuf tells me. And for him, it was an obvious choice to fight in the Iraqi resistance. He considers Bush to be no more of a true Christian than Bin Laden a true Muslim. Real Christians and Muslims do not kill defenseless civilians.

Mosul. 'We do not want to transform our movement into a militia,' he said. 'But if needed, we can arm more than [10,000] people.' "

However, the Christians are in an extremely difficult situation. See in addition: Keller, Gabriela: "Wer bleibt stirbt" *Spiegel Online*, December 1, 2006, www.spiegel. de: "The American invasion in 2003 started a quiet exodus from Iraq. 800,000 people so far have fled from the bloody chaos to Syria. And although Christians account only for four percent of the population, they are more than 30% of the refugees. [...]" [Translation] See also: Thurmann, Michael: Unheilige Schutzmacht. *Die Zeit*, March 23, 2006, http://images.zeit.de/text/2006/13/Syrien: "*Ebtissam* [a female Christian in Iraq] veiled herself carefully so she wouldn't be attacked on the street. 'Shocking to us, because under Saddam Hussein it did not matter if you were Christian or Muslim.' " [Translation]

But at a certain point people who have been robbed of all hope are capable of anything, he admits. Sometimes they find no way out of the vicious circle of violence. That is true, not just of Iraqis, but of all peoples.

Yussuf then cites a passage from the Bible—here in the middle of Iraq—about the siege of Samaria, which was then the capital of the kingdom of Israel: "The famine was so great, that a handful of dove's dung was sold for five silver shekels; and in the end their desperation was so great that some people killed their own sons, cooked and ate them."

"Book of Kings," Yussuf says soberly. There are more passages in the Old Testament about the cannibalism of desperate people, who kill and eat their relatives.

The predicament of his own people is not so different from that of the inhabitants of Samaria in the Kingdom of Israel thousands of years ago. You Westerners, Yussuf tells me, should study your own history before pronouncing judgment over others.

He falls silent. Then he resumes: "There are considerably more Christian resistance fighters in Iraq than Al-Qaeda terrorists. There is no difference between the Christian resistance fighters and their moderate Muslim comrades-in-arms. Christians and Muslims in Iraq belong together and fight together. Nobody in the Iraqi resistance cares whether a fighter is Muslim or Christian."

The Christians of Iraq were one of the most respected Christian communities in the Middle East. Before the American invasion they were much freer than they are today. Even mixed marriages between Muslims and Christians were considered quite normal. But now all that has become impossible.

Christian women now have to wear a veil, because the invasion has allowed Sunni and Shi'ite extremists to surface. The West cannot even imagine what a disaster the United States has created in the once secular state of Iraq—for its Christians inhabitants as well.

"Because most of the American occupation troops are Christian," Yussuf continues, "Al-Qaeda sees Iraq's own Christians as occupiers too. They persecute us. Fortunately, our people often find shelter in the homes of Muslim friends. And Christian families often hide Muslims who are being chased by occupation troops." I look at Yussuf in surprise; he laughs and says it is entirely normal and obvious that they would help each other.

Before the invasion, 1.5 million Christians lived in Iraq. Many were senior figures in the cabinet or the diplomatic service; they were generals, hotel proprietors, or successful businessmen. The former Deputy Prime Minister Tariq Aziz is a practicing Christian.

Now there are only 600,000 Christians here, and their situation is "really lousy." Under the dictatorship of Saddam Hussein things were a lot better for the Christians than they are under the "military dictatorship" of George W. Bush. The U.S. president has launched a very strange kind of "crusade." He is just as much of a terrorist as were the Crusaders of the Middle Ages. That has nothing to do with true Christianity.

Just as the Christians of Iraq fight the "terrorism" of the "Christian" occupiers from the United States, so do the Manichaeans, Sabian Mandaeans and Yezidis. Women also fight in the resistance.

Christians in the resistance are mainly active in Baghdad and Mosul. Christian resistance fighters also sharply condemn suicide and other terrorist attacks in civilians. Terrorism is un-Iraqi, un-Islamic and un-Christian.

Truly free elections can only be held after the Americans pull out. The elections held so far have all been rigged, Yussuf tells me. For the elections in 2004, the names of the candidates were not even disclosed, allegedly for "security reasons." There were only secret lists. The people had no choice but to vote along religious or ethnic lines.

Truckloads of fraudulently completed ballot papers were brought to Baghdad from Iran. It is incredible that nobody in the West expressed surprise that it took two months before the election results were declared.

"How is it possible that you accept such an election, while in Palestine you have them vote as many times as it takes to get the result and the government you want?" asks Yussuf.

He says Saddam Hussein was too harsh a dictator. But the American military dictatorship since the invasion has been much harsher, bloodier and more brutal. "If that is democracy, then you can keep it. Nobody in Iraq could ever have imagined that in the name of democracy the West would torture, rape, mutilate and kill hundreds of thousands of Iraqi civilians.

"And in any case, a democracy in which the people are bamboozled about important issues is not a true democracy. How can a state claim to uphold the rule of law and at the same time willfully break international law? That is fraud! It makes me sick," Yussuf declares, "to think that the U.S. president claims, as a born-again Christian, to be acting in the name of God."

"I too," he says, "am a Christian."

Yussuf stands up to leave: "Tell your people in Germany that it is not only Muslims who are fighting the United States in Iraq, but Christians as well. We want to be free, free of Western occupation forces and free of Western terrorism. That holds for us Christians as well." He bows and departs with a brief smile, leaving me feeling thoughtful and rattled.

Rami

I am exhausted, and so is Abu Saeed, despite the countless glasses of tea he has drunk. It is much too hot in this room. Abu Saeed sees that I have heard and seen enough for one day and that I am completely worn out. Still, he says there is one more resistance fighter I have to meet today.

Before I can respond, he is at the door, beckoning to someone to come in. Rami enters and sits down opposite me. He is a slender young man of 27, with short hair and a smart chin beard.

Rami's face is gray, his expression bitter. By day he studies history at the University of Baghdad. By night he fights the U.S. Army. When I ask him why, his expression becomes even more bitter. In a quiet voice he starts to tell me his story.

A few months after the American invasion, U.S. soldiers stormed his family's house. They called it a "cleansing operation." They smashed everything that crossed their path. They were looking for him, Rami tells me, because somebody had told them that he was working for the resistance. But at that time he had nothing at all to do with it. The soldiers could not find him, so they started pulling apart the closets and turning the whole house upside down.

His mother was crying and threw herself at the feet of the soldiers, pleading with them not to destroy her family's few possessions. One of the soldiers took a step back and shot her dead.

Rami purses his lips and falls silent. When he has regained his composure, he struggles for words as he tells me that is what the occupation troops often do. If they don't find the person they are looking for, they shoot a member of his family or put his relatives in prison.

If I don't believe him, Rami says, I should read the story of Abeer, the girl from Mahmudiyah who was raped and then killed along with her family by members of a U.S. military unit.[13] That is just one example of the brutality of the occupation troops. Rami stops talking and remains silent for several minutes.

Then, haltingly, he resumes. Such things are usually hushed up. The perpetrators are only prosecuted if some courageous journalist brings an atrocity to the public's attention. Rami says he doubts he will ever smile again. The American soldiers have shot the smile out of his heart and his face.

Then he utters a sentence I never wanted to be confronted with in Iraq. Just thinking about it as I prepared for this journey sent shivers down my spine. And now Rami says to me: "And that is why I fight for Al-Qaeda."

I look at Abu Saeed in fury and tell him he knew full well that I wanted to have nothing to do with Al-Qaeda. Abu Saeed looks back at me with an innocent expression and reminds me that I had said I wanted to meet a representative cross-section of all the groups fighting in Iraq, and that is what he is providing me with. Except for the Shi'ite militias. He can't help me there.

Al-Qaeda is, unfortunately, part of the post-war reality in Iraq, he continues. One that has been imported by the United States. "You wanted to see what the invasion has done to Iraq.

"That is why I have introduced you to an Al-Qaeda fighter. The presence of Al-Qaeda in Iraq is one of the consequences of the American invasion. Under Saddam Hussein every religious extremist was persecuted—perhaps, in your view, too mercilessly. But under Saddam, Al-Qaeda would not have stood a chance in Iraq."

Rami has not understood what we were saying, but he has guessed that we were talking about him and about Al-Qaeda. I do not know what to do. I had wanted to avoid this situation for many reasons, including concern for my own personal safety. But now I am in that situation, and cannot pretend this conversation is not happening.

We are all on our feet, but now I sit down again and gesture to Rami to do the same. I ask him why on earth he would be so crazy as to join such a gang of murderers, who have killed thousands of civilians and brought dishonor and disrespect upon Islam. Rami looks at me calmly and asks: "What would you have done if your mother had been killed in front of her family?"

I say I do not know, but that I surely would not have joined a terrorist organization. Rami answers quietly that he had had three options: to join either the anti-colonialist 1920 Revolutionary Brigades or the Ba'athists or Al-Qaeda. His father and brother chose the Ba'athists; he chose Al-Qaeda.

He received military training from an old army officer. In

his own home the officer taught Rami and two friends the basics about bombs with timed detonators, ground-to-ground missiles, remote-controlled explosive devices—things he had known nothing about before.

Rami says he is fighting for an Islamic Iraq with a constitution based on the Qur'an and with respect for the sharia. But if the Ba'athists or other resistance groups were to win elections, he would respect any government they formed.

Rami notices that I am still looking angry and says he belongs to the moderate wing of Al-Qaeda, like most Iraqi members and fighters. He says he has never killed a civilian and will never do so. But the United States must stop tormenting and abusing his country.

Germany too is now playing a tragic part—especially in Afghanistan—even though it took such a clear stand on the Iraq war. Rami asks me whether I had ever considered the fact that NATO, with German support, had killed more civilians in Afghanistan than the Taliban had done.

I reply that even if this well-known propaganda claim by Al-Qaeda were true, which is something I cannot judge, that would still be no reason to join a terrorist organization like Al-Qaeda. Our discussion becomes more heated. Rami says again that moderate members of Al-Qaeda really do exist. These members, including himself, reject violence against civilians. Violence against civilians, even against "decent Iraqi police officers," is not acceptable even if at the same time American soldiers are killed.

Why then, I ask him, did he join Al-Qaeda? That means at the very least being an accessory to terrorism. Rami does not give me a straight answer. He says he repeatedly objected to the radical, foreign wing of Al-Qaeda, but neither he nor his friends had any influence. His opinion was respected, but not accepted.

He knows that the extremists take hostages, kill civilians and have an extremely narrow view of the world. He does not accept that but he still supports Al-Qaeda because it is most active in fighting the occupiers.

I ask him what he thinks of Al-Zarqawi and Bin Laden. Rami again astonishes me with the inconsistency of his arguments. He says he admires both men. He would have liked to work with Al-Zarqawi because he inflicted heavy losses on U.S. forces. Rami says he is impressed by Bin Laden's courage in standing up to the United States.

We have reached a point at which I feel it makes no sense to continue talking. It is hopeless, talking to followers of Al-Zarqawi and Bin Laden. I stand up to indicate the meeting is over. Rami also rises.

His argumentation is entirely irrational. And he knows it. He rejects violence against civilians and admires terrorists who mercilessly murder innocent civilians. Rami sees that I do not want to ask him any more questions. But he tries again to justify his position.

Rami tells me that he used to be a quiet and peaceable student. But then he experienced the daily humiliation of his people; he saw the images from Abu Ghraib on television and the Internet. After the death of his mother he could not sleep or eat for days.

Although he had never been a supporter of the Ba'athist Party, he cried when he saw Saddam Hussein's execution on television. Saddam was not a good ruler, but under him there was security and peace. The chaos in Iraq shows that the country needs a strong leader. Rami asks me whether occupation by the Americans and chaos are really better than Saddam Hussein's dictatorship.

I say neither the one nor the other is right. But Rami just keeps on talking. He was never a particularly devout Muslim, he says, but the invasion by the Americans and the atrocities they commit, which are a thousand times worse than those blamed on Al-Qaeda, have turned him into a patriot and a Muslim. In fact, many Iraqis only became patriotic and religious in response to the occupation.

Bush is responsible for the deaths of many more people than all the dictators and terrorists in the world put together. Nonetheless, every Western politician is proud to have a meeting with Bush. Rami snarls in anger: "Your politicians count the minutes they are allowed to spend with the American president, and nobody holds him to account for the death of hundreds of thousands of Iraqis."

He knows that he is on the U.S. forces' wanted list, but he does not care. He is not afraid to die. Why should he fare better than his mother or his friends or the many other Iraqis who have lost their lives over the past four years? He will never forget the suffering that the Americans have inflicted on his family and his friends. Never, ever!

At this point, I knew I should definitely bring our conversation to an end, but I find Rami interesting—this sad, bitter, helpless, ashen-faced man, who looks nothing like the stereotype of a terrorist. So I let him continue telling me his story.

Like most of his fellow fighters he has also been in prison. He says he was well treated "physically." But "psychologically" he was humiliated. They locked him in a tiny cell of not more than two square meters. And like many other prisoners he was forced to go naked to interrogations.

Nonetheless, he does not feel hatred for the Americans. He does not know them. He cannot say whether they are good or bad. He only hates what they did to his family and what they are doing to his people; he hates the chaos into which they have plunged his country.

The death squads of Shi'ite politicians can only commit their murders because the United States allow them to. Why do I only protest against Al-Qaeda and not against the murdering Americans? His murdered relatives were also civilians.

I do not reply, and Rami continues. His family has less and less to eat. Under the UN sanction regime, there was not enough to eat either, but now the situation is catastrophic, at least for his family. The food distribution points for Sunnis are often in neighborhoods controlled by Shi'ite militia. Sometimes people go hungry for weeks on end.

These are all reasons why he is fighting with Al-Qaeda for the liberation of Iraq. The United States has destroyed everything he loves. He did not choose to be in this situation, and he doubts whether I really understand how much his people are suffering.

It is easy to pass judgment on resistance and terrorism if you are living in peace and prosperity. But he sees nothing but suffering, misery, humiliation, blood and death around him, Rami explains. Have I ever thought about what young people must have gone through, if they come to see no alternative but to blow themselves up? Then Rami says: "Stop attacking us and humiliating us. Get out of our country. Then Al-Qaeda will disappear all by itself." Rami turns around abruptly and leaves the room.

I remain alone with Abu Saeed in the dark room. I know that people in Western countries will attack me for talking to members of Al-Qaeda. They will not, for the most part, be very interested in the fact that some Al-Qaeda fighters consider themselves to be moderate. But how can one fight this terrorist madness if one does not investigate it and try to understand the terrorists' motivation?

One reason why the counter-terrorism policies of the West have failed over the past few years is that most politicians have not adequately researched and addressed the phenomenon of terrorism. The Baker-Hamilton Report reaches the sardonic conclusion that while the United States knows all about the explosive devices used against its troops, it knows next to nothing about the people who set off those devices or their motives.*

When I was a young judge I was involved for a few months in the trial of a terrorist, a member of the Red Army Faction. German terrorists killed a great friend of mine, Hanns Martin Schleyer, who was like a father to me. And when I was a young-

---

* Baker-Hamilton Report (2006), p. 61: The Defense Department and the intelligence community have not invested sufficient people and resources to understand the political and military threat to American men and women in the armed forces. Congress has appropriated almost $2 billion this year for countermeasures to protect our troops in Iraq against improvised explosive devices, but the administration has not put forward a request to invest comparable resources in trying to understand the people who fabricate, plant, and explode those devices.

ster, I was well acquainted with someone who later turned into a terrorist. I have thought long and hard about the phenomenon of terrorism.

The main cause of terrorism is not need or poverty, but the perception that there is no way to remedy a situation regarded to be deeply unjust by legal means. Terrorism is the supreme expression of despair. The only effective strategy to combat terrorism must be a combination of stringency and fairness, serving both impartial principles and justice. Stringency alone is not sufficient. Without justice one cannot overcome terrorism.

Abu Saeed sees that I am deep in thought and full of doubts. "Let's go," he says, "and don't be angry because you talked to somebody from Al-Qaeda. We have to talk to them. We have to beat the extremists and drive them from our country; the moderates among them we have to win over."

Zaid is standing outside and stares at me with an inquisitive look on his face. He had sat the whole time with the men Abu Saeed had brought for me to meet. I tell him the conversations were very interesting. I had learned a lot, but there were things I could not confirm or check. I would have needed to spend more time with them in order to really understand what they feel and what they do. And I tell Zaid that I need his help.

The expression in his face again becomes distant. It is quite clear that he does not want to disclose the most painful chapters of his life. I ask him what he thinks of Al-Qaeda. "The foreign Al-Qaeda fighters are murderers," he says. "For Iraq, they are just as bad as the Americans. We have to drive them out of the country as well." We return to Al-Jazeera in silence.

Jubilation in Ramadi

Back at Abu Saeed's house, the whole family is again sitting in front of the television. The Iraqi national soccer team is on its victory tour of neighboring countries. In Dubai and Jordan, the squad receives a rousing welcome from thousands of exiled Iraqis.

The decisive goals are shown for the 100th time—the ones that led to the final and then the clincher that won Iraq the Asian Cup. The final was played five days ago, but Abu Saeed's extended family still can't get enough of it. Zaid also likes to look at the footage of Iraq's one and only international victory in years.

The current Iraqi government has never once managed to bring a smile to people's faces, Zaid tells me, and we can never decide if it is Iran or the United States that is pulling its strings. But the Iraqi soccer team has filled the hearts of all Iraqis with joy and, magically, even brought a smile to the saddest faces.

Right after the final whistle, the whole of Ramadi rushed out onto the streets. Thousands were dancing, singing and celebrating. In a break with tradition, though, nobody fired into the air. That would have been just a little too dangerous. Who knows if the Americans would not have fired back, like they do at wedding parties in Afghanistan.

The Iraqi police and the Iraqi Army also joined in the celebrations. When an American Humvee patrol came by, people blocked its path, with the approval of Iraqi police officers. One American Humvee driver got out and started to dance with the crowd. A little boy picked up a piece of melon rind and threw it at his head. The American quickly got back into his vehicle. This was the Iraqis' party, not the Americans, Zaid says with a laugh.

I ask him who his favorite soccer player is. Without hesitation he fires back: "Zinedine Zidane. He is the greatest, and he is an Arab and a Muslim."

"But what about that head butt during the World Cup final between France and Italy?" I ask. Zaid says he did not think that was right, nor did his friends. But when he heard that the Italian player Materazzi was said to have insulted Zidane's mother and sister and called him an Arab terrorist, then they could all sympathize with Zidane.

"You know," Zaid says, "sometimes you have it up to here; it is the last straw which breaks a camels back. What Materazzi did to Zidane is what the West does with us Arabs all the time." Zidane's head butt has a symbolic meaning. "But you Westerners wouldn't understand that."

It is now 10 o'clock in the evening and the women of the house have prepared another delicious meal and served it outside the house on the lawn. We enjoy the food in silence. Zaid is going to spend the night here with us. We stay up late talking, not about politics or war, but about soccer. Suddenly, Zaid is once again a carefree, cheerful youngster, like millions of other boys around the world when they talk about soccer.

By the time I finally lie down on my foam mattress, it is 1 a.m. Abu Saeed, Abu Hamid and Zaid are still playing dominoes. Apart from that, everything is just as usual: the power is out again, the two American helicopters have flown over the house a number of times, an American reconnaissance plane circles above the so-called "Sunni Triangle"; the sky is full of twinkling stars, the moon shines through the crown of the tall palms; and I am yearning for five sweet hours of deep sleep—insha'Allah!

Zaid's Brothers

I only manage four hours. At 5 a.m. the call of the muezzin awakens me. I want to turn round and go right back to sleep, but Abu Saeed asks me to get up right away. He looks tense. We have to leave the house by 10 at the latest, he says. If I want to talk to Zaid today, I must rise immediately.

In Ramadi, word has got out that a Westerner is staying in Al-Jazeera. Abu Saeed has heard from friends in the police force that something is in the air. He cannot rule out the possibility that there might still be a few scattered Al-Qaeda terrorists in Ramadi. And if the Americans hear about me being here, that could spell serious trouble for Abu Saeed and his family.

The Americans would find it very suspicious that there is a Westerner in Ramadi, without permission from the Pentagon, who is talking to people who have not been briefed in advance. It is very unusual and does not fit with their PR strategy. That is why we should go and stay somewhere else for a while.

I get up without saying a word and shuffle like a boxer after a knockout to the shower, where a large mug of coffee is waiting for me. By 5:30 a.m., Zaid and I are sitting under a date palm and he is talking. The day is slowly dawning. Zaid has dark rings under his eyes. Perhaps he has not slept but was thinking all night about what he and his family have gone through in recent months.

Zaid talks very slowly and deliberately today. He is clearly try-ing to keep his emotions under control. He often breathes deeply, pauses, and purses his lips.

Zaid is the oldest of three brothers. Haroun is one year young-er, and Karim two years his junior. In July 2006, Haroun spends a few nights at his uncle's house in the center of Ramadi. He is 19 at the time and studying engineering. It is summer break, and he is trying to enjoy it as best he can, given a war is underway.

Like his two brothers, he has little to do with the resistance. Though like all the youngsters in Ramadi, he helps the resistance fighters when they are looking for a hideout or need information. But Haroun does not play an active part.

On July 14, 2006, Haroun sets off early in the morning, be-fore it gets too hot, from his uncle's house to go back to his family in Al-Sufia. He turns into the long and narrow street where his family lives, it is just after seven o'clock a.m. He is dribbling a ball he found on the way.

In his right hand he is carrying a white bush rose which he picked for his mother at sunrise. He sees a young neighbor, Jarir, coming the other way, and calls out to greet him, "salam—peace."

Just as he utters the word *salam*, a shot rings out. Haroun touches the back of his head in disbelief, sinks to his knees in what seems like slow motion, and falls forwards with his face hitting the dust.

His lifeless body lies there in the dirt, the small white rose he selected for his mother in his right hand.

Jarir had darted for cover into the entry of an abandoned house. He stands there for hours without moving. One hour after the shooting, he sees a municipal fire truck come to collect Haroun's body and take it away. Fire trucks are the only vehicles allowed to drive in the city center. Even ambulances get shot at immediately. So fire trucks now also function as ambulances and hearses.

Other people living on the street heard the shot too, but nobody dared go out to see, scared of becoming the American snipers next target.

Jarir only dares to leave his hiding place in the afternoon. He runs to Zaid's house and tells the family that Haroun has been shot. Cries of despair, mourning and anger fill the house. Weeping and wailing, the members of his family cling to each other. It is stupefying that Haroun is dead. They saw him only yesterday at his uncle's house.

The entire family then goes to the district morgue to see Haroun one last time, to say goodbye and to prepare the funeral. But when they get there, they discover Haroun has already been buried. Without a steady supply of electricity, the morgue cannot use its cold-storage facility; so the many corpses that are brought there daily have to be buried as quickly as possible.

The family cannot say goodbye or perform the prescribed prayers that are customary at a burial. Perhaps nobody said them for Haroun. Zaid's parents, his two sisters, Lamya and Maysun, Zaid and Karim walk home, crying and holding each other tight.

Zaid stops talking. I sense that he needs a break. He has put his hands over his eyes to hide his tears. His whole body shakes as he sobs. I get up and leave him alone for a few minutes. After he has regained his composure, I go back to Zaid. He looks exhausted, but he resumes his account.

Although Zaid and his 18-year-old brother Karim feel over-whelmingly sad for weeks as they mourn Haroun, they decide to concentrate on their studies. Karim has just completed his high school diploma and wants to study agriculture.

Zaid and Karim grow closer during this period. Zaid takes Karim along to games of soccer and tries to make sure they always play on the same team. Sometimes he even misses soccer prac-tice to go swimming with Karim in the Euphrates, because Karim loves swimming so much.

In the fall, their studies resume. Zaid sees to it that the two do their homework together in the afternoons. Whenever Karim stares into the distance with blank eyes, Zaid knows that he is thinking of Haroun. Zaid then often tells Karim a funny story.

Weeks and months pass. In early 2007, heavy fighting erupts in Ramadi again. Zaid's family home is not damaged, but on January 5th, in the evening, a missile fired from an American helicopter hits right beside the house and destroys a generator that provided electricity to their house and some others nearby.

The panic-stricken family keep their heads down, run away from the fighting as fast as they can. They walk to the house of an uncle a few hundred meters away. Arriving completely out of breath, they suddenly realize that they had forgotten to turn off the kerosene heaters. Karim decides he will run back.

He opens the door and looks cautiously right and left to see if the coast is clear. As he runs off, Zaid calls after him: "Be careful!" At that moment there is a burst of machine-gun fire in the road. Less than 30 meters from their uncle's house, Karim collapses, riddled by American bullets.

Zaid is about to dash out and rescue Karim, but his sisters hold him back. Zaid hates violence; he never got into fights at school and he never commits a foul in soccer; but now something snaps inside him.

Shrieking with pain and fury, Zaid is determined to go out and fetch the body of his little brother lying in a large pool of blood in the middle of the road. And he wants to go after the Americans—and kill at least one with his bare hands, even though bursts of machine-gun fire still resound outside.

His father holds Zaid back, his mother grabs his T-shirt and will not let go. They all clasp each other tight; the whole family is wailing and crying in despair. Zaid beats the wall with his fists and sobs: "I have to go and get my brother, perhaps he is still alive." But his parents and his sister are terrified of losing Zaid as well and do not let him go.

The whole night the family looks out through the small kitchen window. Just a few meters away Karim is lying in the dark pool of his blood. Gunfire continues. Shots hit the door of the house. It is impossible to retrieve Karim's body.

At about nine in the morning the fire truck arrives. Shielded by its bulk, the family rushes out into the road, but it is much too late. Zaid carefully lifts the body of his little brother and carries it to the fire truck. He lays it on a stretcher in the back of the vehicle and sits down beside the body, rests his head on Karim's chest, and starts to cry.

Zaid's eyes fill with tears, and I put my hand on his shoulder. He looks past me, as tears roll down his cheeks. I am about to leave him alone again, but he holds me tight, takes a couple of deep breaths, and carries on telling me his story. He wants to get it over and done with now.

His lips quiver, he runs his hands through his thick hair. The wounds left by Karim's death seven months ago have not healed.

Zaid and his family accompany Karim in the fire truck to a mosque, where they recite the Islamic prayers for the dead. At midday, they bury him. Despondent and empty, they walk home. Zaid's father looks frail and walks slowly. He has aged by years in this one night.

Zaid's family could not bury Karim next to Haroun. The rules imposed by the occupying power would not permit them to drive to the district where Haroun is buried. The rules are strict; special wishes are not considered.

What happened on the night of January 5, 2007, did not only change Zaid's father, but Zaid as well. It has transformed him. He tells me quietly that after the death of his little brother he realized that it was not enough to just support the resistance passively. He comes to the conclusion that he must do more—like most of his friends.

The number of dead in Ramadi is now in the thousands. Almost every family has lost somebody. "Do you know that they have turned the soccer pitches into cemeteries in Ramadi?" he asks me. "There isn't enough room in the designated cemeteries."

Zaid despises Al-Qaeda, because not only does it fight the Americans in Ramadi, but also anyone who tries to stand up to it—ordinary people, tribal leaders, physicians, engineers and workers. And it does so with great brutality. So he could only consider joining the moderate Islamist resistance movements, independent nationalist organizations or the Ba'athist resistance. Zaid finds it hard to make up his mind; he has no clear preference. He just knows that he must do something.

At the Center of the Resistance

Abu Saeed has been standing behind us in silence for some minutes. "We have to go," he says, "otherwise we could be in trouble, and we still have a lot to do." It is 9:30 a.m.

I pack my things and throw them in the back of the car. Zaid comes with us. Abu Saeed asks me to cover my head in the traditional Arab way with a *ghutra* and *agal*, a headscarf held in place with a thick black cord.

We drive along bumpy lanes and potholed roads towards the center of town. We go through countless checkpoints. Seated in the back of the Chevrolet with tinted windows, wearing Arab dress, I remain inconspicuous. My dapper moustache proves useful, though it is starting to tickle annoyingly.

Downtown Ramadi is closed to cars; at the point where people and goods transfer to small brightly painted *tartorahs* or tricycles, we turn into a side street lined with houses that look like villas. As Moussa slows down in front of one of the houses, the large garden gate opens as if by magic, we turn in, and the gate closes at once behind us.

A number of dignified looking men aged between 40 and 60 welcome me at the door. They and I are all wearing white dishdashas and ghutras with black agals.

Abu Saeed tells me in a whisper that they are top-level leaders of the resistance in Anbar province. The oldest, Abu Bassim, used to be a four-star general. Abu Saeed does not reveal which of the five is the commander-in-chief; I have to find that out for myself. Abu Bassim is just the host.

We enter a cool room. The air conditioning is powered by the house's own generator. It is so effective that I am freezing. Abu Bassim, who like his colleagues, changes residence every few weeks as a security precaution, offers me an armchair next to the air conditioning unit. The curtains are drawn to keep out the sun, and perhaps for security reasons as well.

Once my eyes have adjusted to the dim light, I see lying on a simple bed a man of about 30 with a big head and a crew cut. I go over to talk to him. His name is Samir, and he is paralyzed from the waist down. While the commanders of the resistance in Anbar province talk quietly with Abu Saeed, Samir tells me how he came to be severely injured.

In early 2006, he was driving with his friend Yaser in his Mitsubishi on a country road from Ramadi towards Baghdad, where they were going to visit a physician. As they were passing through a village, they suddenly got caught in a traffic jam; Yaser had to stop in the middle of a crossroads. At that moment an armored Humvee appeared out of the side road and rammed the Mitsubishi. The car was pushed off the road, overturned and totally wrecked. Yaser was killed at once; and he, Samir, was trapped between the passenger seat and the dashboard.

The armored Humvee was not even damaged. Its driver backed up and then drove off, without paying any further attention to the people in the wrecked Mitsubishi. Samir never found out who the driver of the Humvee was.

They had to use a welding torch to free him from the Mitsubishi, Samir tells me. In the hospital they tell him the fifth of his thoracic vertebras has been smashed and he will remain paralyzed for the rest of his life. He thinks every day of his dead friend. But his own body is dead as well.

I ask him if he had been active in the resistance. He laughs and says that almost every Iraqi is in the resistance but that he had not been active as a fighter. Some of his cousins joined right at the start. Nine of them were locked up in Abu Ghraib prison in 2004 as a consequence. Four were killed when an attempt was made to free them that September. During the fighting, the Americans had taken them as a cover and simply used them as human shields.

They held him as well, for a month and a half in Abu Ghraib in 2004, Samir tells me. "We were treated like animals.

"They beat us, kicked us and spat at us. There was loud noise day and night. They wanted to force us to eat pork, which the Qur'an forbids and we did not touch it. So for days we had nothing to eat."

About 60 of his relatives have been killed so far—brothers and sisters, uncles, cousins. But who cares about that in the West? There they count the dead Americans very carefully, no one bothers any more to count the dead Iraqis properly.

The fact that Al-Qaeda and radical Shi'ite militias have killed many Iraqi civilians does not in any way absolve the United States of their liability. "The Americans have brought these plagues down upon our country. They bear the responsibility. Before the

Americans marched in, there were no terrorists in our country and no sectarian violence."

Twelve people have now gathered in the large living room, and the mood is bitter. As host, Abu Bassim now formally welcomes me in the name of his family and friends. He says, I am the first Westerner who did not come to Ramadi in an American helicopter, Humvee or armored personnel carrier and the first to come without a press officer or military bodyguards and the first who does not spend his nights in a fortified American army camp. For that he offers me his sincere thanks.

It means that I at least have a chance, Abu Bassim continues, to discover the truth. He is amazed that so many Western journalists rely on military officers to tell them about the situation of the people in Iraq. It is obvious that the Pentagon does not want to reveal the true extent of the tragedy.

Imagine if a journalist accompanying German troops in occupied Poland in 1943 wrote about the situation of the Polish population on the basis of what he was told by a German press officer, says Abu Bassim.

I tell him that for most correspondents being an "embedded journalist" is the only way to get to see Iraq at all; that is just the way it is in occupied countries.

He replies calmly that I am proof that there are indeed alternatives. But, I tell him, I could not make such a trip several times a year and that I probably do not get to see everything either; I also have to make many compromises.

Abu Bassim says: "That is true, but you have come to see the victims of this war; almost all the others visit the perpetrators."

That means the Pentagon has in effect a monopoly on information. Not a single journalist has spoken to the resistance in Ramadi over the past four and a half years. Many do not even know that such a resistance movement exists, even though it is second only to American forces here in Iraq in terms of military might.

"Reports from the front" in Ramadi published in the international press are often identical, down to the last detail. Reporters often just pass on verbatim what American press officers tell them, so they rave about all the improvements in the supply of electricity, water and gas, though in fact the opposite is the case. These journalists do not spend any time with real Iraqi families. They just repeat what they are being told by the American officers at their side. And those officers have never really spent some time with ordinary Iraqi families either. This kind of reporting is ridiculous.

The rosy picture the Pentagon presents to the media of the situation in certain Iraqi cities, especially in recent months, does not correspond to reality, and will not do so for a long time. There has been too much pain and suffering, not just in Ramadi, but across Iraq.

I tell Abu Bassim that I think his criticism is too sweeping; I have read many well-informed and fair-minded articles about Iraq, in the German and in the American press. For me, the "embedded journalists" are for the most part particularly courageous reporters. They risk their life to do their job. Almost 200 journalists have already been killed in Iraq.

At the same time, I think to myself that his criticism is in part justified. Many media outlets are not critical and discerning enough of statements from the Pentagon; and my method of gathering information, which Abu Bassim so welcomes, will cause me no end of problems when I get back home.

I change the subject and ask him about the military situation in Ramadi. Abu Bassim tells me that after the fall of Fallujah, most of which was reduced to rubble by U.S. bombing in 2004, Ramadi became the center of the Iraqi resistance. And apart from a few neighborhoods, the entire city came under the control of the resistance. The 450,000 residents supported the resistance from the start. The American General James Mattis once said that the whole region would go to hell if Ramadi fell.[14]

Morale among the American occupation troops was bad from the start. His tribe helped a number of American soldiers desert, and smuggled them across the border into Jordan. The GIs paid an average of 600 dollars just to get out of Iraq. And they had to hand over their uniforms and weapons. But they were happy to do so. In exchange they were given an Iraqi dishdasha.

Abu Bassim says he himself helped five American soldiers flee. They came to an agreed meeting point in their Humvees, got out, changed their clothes, and handed over their weapons and 600 dollars. After dark they were taken to Jordan. The next morning helicopters flew over the Humvees several times, and when the crews failed to establish contact with the GIs, they bombed the Humvees.

The unusually high suicide rate among American soldiers after they return home also indicates what a devastating experience the mad war in Iraq is for many.[15] There have been reports on this phenomenon in the American and Arab media. The number of such suicides is considerably higher than the number of American soldiers actually killed in Iraq.

There were fierce battles around Ramadi for two and a half years. The Americans launched several major offensives in June 2006. They stormed hundreds of houses, in order to "cleanse" them and take "insurgents and terrorists" prisoner, as they put it. They were unimaginably brutal. They often blew out the doors with grenades. For months there was fighting in the streets of Ramadi.

The city was also subjected to aerial bombardment. Parts of its center came to resemble Beirut after the civil war. In November 2006, countless civilians were killed in bombing raids—some just were sitting at an Internet café. Many women and children were among the victims.

As usual, the U.S. forces initially denied that. When photos of the bodies surfaced, they started talking about unavoidable collateral damage. In his estimation, Abu Bassim continues, one has to multiply by at least 10 the Iraqi casualty figures released by the Pentagon to get anywhere close to the truth.

The resistance in Ramadi was far superior to the U.S. troops. In late 2006, the American press published secret Pentagon reports that stated that the United States had lost Ramadi and that the marines didn't stand a chance against the "insurgents"; the two-and-a-half-year battle for Ramadi was lost.

Unfortunately, its significance as a center of the Iraqi resistance and its relative proximity to Baghdad also attracted Al-Qaeda to Ramadi.[16] Al-Qaeda fighters came in droves, and have done terrible damage. The Jordanian Al-Zarqawi spent a lot of time in Ramadi and the surrounding area. In its megalomania, Al-Qaeda even declared Ramadi the center of the liberated "Islamic Republic of Iraq."

Hundreds of Al-Qaeda terrorists joined the fighting in Ramadi. In the early days, there was some limited cooperation between the Iraqi resistance and Al-Qaeda. But then Al-Qaeda besmirched the honor of the Iraqi resistance, both here and in Baghdad. Its commandos did not only shoot at the enemy, but would fire indiscriminately at civilians as well. They turned Ramadi into Iraq's Wild West.

The resistance has always been proud of its commitment to spare civilians. "This young man is a fine example of that," Abu Bassim says as he points to Zaid, who blushes deeply. It is obvious that even the leadership of the resistance has heard the story of Zaid aborting a remote-control detonation because an old man was near where the explosive device was intended to go off.

On YouTube you can see footage of a similar event, he says. A resistance fighter has an American soldier in his sights; every time he is about to pull the trigger, he sees a child running past the soldier. After a few minutes the resistance fighter gives up. If I want to, he will show me the clip, Abu Bassim says. I note once again that the Internet revolution has also reached Iraq.

None of his people is permitted to kill civilians, while the foreign fighters of Al-Qaeda do so mercilessly and without restraint. For him, Abu Bassim continues, this is the borderline between resistance and terrorism. Al-Qaeda and the militias that kill civilians are quite simply murderers. Al-Qaeda has been responsible for almost 10 percent of the civilian deaths in Ramadi—the rate here is probably higher than in other parts of the country.

The city's resistance groups and the tribal elders of Anbar agreed to take on these mostly foreign murderers and to drive them out of Ramadi. About half the tribes even decided to call a temporary ceasefire with the Americans in order to pursue that goal. Of course, that also involved a lot of dollars changing hands.

In June 2007, a conference was held on this issue at the Mansour Melia Hotel, near the Green Zone in Baghdad. Some tribal elders from Anbar took part. A bomb attack aimed at the participants of the conference killed twelve people.[17]

As that attack demonstrates, many people were opposed to the local deals made in Anbar with the Americans. The only point on which all agree is the need to fight Al-Qaeda.

I suddenly remember that my original plan was to visit Baghdad in June 2007, and that in my visa application I had given the Mansour Melia Hotel as the place where I would be staying. "That was a close shave," I think to myself.

Abu Bassim continues: "The strategy of focusing on Al-Qaeda paid off. The worst Al-Qaeda terrorists, almost all foreigners, were chased away. It happened quite fast." The people of Ramadi simply showed Al-Qaeda the red card. Nowhere in the world can guerrilla fighters survive without popular support.

In the other provinces of Iraq as well, more and more people reject Al-Qaeda. Iraqi members are leaving it in droves. The totalitarian inhuman ideology of this terrorist organization is completely alien to Iraqis. "The Iraqis are fed up with Al-Qaeda," says Abu Bassim. "We also want to liberate our country ourselves. We do not need the help of any foreign fanatics."

Abu Bassim says he knows that the ceasefire also gave the U.S. troops a breather, but that was a price worth paying to increase the safety of the civilian population, which had been worn down and exhausted by American bombing raids and the senseless killing sprees of Al-Qaeda terrorists.

There have been such ceasefires in the history of all liberation movements the world over. They give the resistance an opportunity to regroup and organize. Resistance is not homogenous or continuous, but ebbs and flows. America should have learnt this lesson from Vietnam.

The resistance did not care that the U.S. government sold this ceasefire to the world media as one of its great successes, Abu Bassim continues. "We know that the Pentagon flies entire press delegations into the center of Ramadi to show off success at last."

What the Pentagon does not show the journalists they invite to Ramadi is the "four kilometer zone," protected by armored Humvees and hermetically sealed by American and Iraqi security forces—an area in which they can move freely. To get through the security ring to enter the zone, you have to show your papers at countless police and military checkpoints. It takes hours. Sometimes you just do not get through at all.

"But these flaunting PR events do not interest us: We shall never accept the American occupation," says Abu Bassim. "Almost each Iraqi demands the withdrawal of the U.S. armed forces. Time is on our side, not on the American side. We had to endure the British for many years after the First World War. The Americans will have to depart much quicker—and way sooner than they can imagine.

"The Iraqi resistance is everywhere and nowhere. We strike

when and where we choose. It could be tomorrow in Ramadi, or in one year from now. We know that we shall win this war. And the Americans know that they have lost it and have to leave. Eventually, perhaps tomorrow, perhaps the day after tomorrow— insha'Allah!"

I ask Abu Bassim whether Iraqis also share responsibility for the horrible terrorist violence that the world sees almost every evening on the television news. Abu Bassim nods. There are indeed some Iraqi terrorists as well, he concedes. "In Al-Qaeda and in the militias."

The occupiers and their agents, however, are directly responsible for half the violent deaths in Iraq—a fact that many like to overlook. Abu Bassim estimates that a further 30 percent are the work of the Shi'ite militias, between 5 and 10 percent that of Al-Qaeda, and that the private U.S. "security contractors" and common Iraqi criminals are responsible for the rest. Nobody has precise figures.[18]

The policies of the occupiers and the terrorism and the suffering they have caused have also led to "ethnic cleansing." Sunnis are driven out of mainly Shi'ite areas, and Shi'ites out of Sunni regions. In Anbar province as well, Al-Qaeda drove Shi'ites out of some villages. There are things of which he as an Iraqi cannot be proud of, Abu Bassim tells me.

He points out, however, that under international law the occupying forces are responsible for the security of the population. "We have not created this catastrophic situation. The United States bear the legal and moral responsibility—and not only for those 50 percent they kill themselves." Almost all the terrorist suicide attacks, which the international community rightly deplores, are masterminded abroad—by Al-Qaeda and Iran, but also by paid agents of the United States.

For example, Abu Bassim continues, he knows an Iraqi translator who worked for a long time for U.S. troops, American intelligence and for Blackwater. At some point a dispute erupted, which led to the loss of mutual trust. So the translator was very surprised when one day a go-between of the Americans came to him and asked him to go to Kirkuk in an official car and to meet an Iraqi contact there near the market square. He was told to call a certain number on his cell phone as soon as he reached the square for further instructions.

The translator set off for Kirkuk, pleased to have been offered more work despite the earlier falling out. On the way he started thinking about the strange instructions. So instead of calling the given number from the market place in Kirkuk, he parked the car on an empty construction site and walked several hundred meters away before calling the number.

As he pressed the green call button, the car exploded. There was a huge cloud of flames and smoke. If he had called from the market place as he had been told to do, he would have been killed, along with countless innocent people.

And the media would have reported that another Iraqi suicide bomber had blown himself up at a crowded market. The spiral of hatred between the different communities would have intensified further. The translator never contacted his former employers again and now works in the resistance—under his command, Abu Bassim tells me.

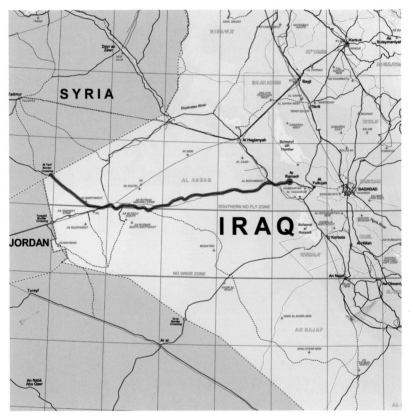

1. The author's route between Ramadi and Syria.

2. January 2003, a couple of weeks before the war, Jürgen Todenhöfer's second trip to Iraq. Children on "Blacksmith Road" in Baghdad.

3. No photos! American armored personnel carrier on its way to Jordan. The author is on the left.

4. On the side of the street to Ramadi: passenger bus, destroyed by American armed forces.

5. The armored personnel carrier is followed by a Humvee.

6. Road blocks on the way to the center of Ramadi.

7. House on 20th street in Ramadi, destroyed by an air raid.

8. Al-Sufia: the destroyed generator next to Zaid's house.

9. Ramadi, August 2007. Dinner with the leaders of the moderate Islamic and national resistance of Anbar province.

10. Followed by nightly prayers. Abu Saeed leads the prayers.

11. The author in Abu Saeed's guest room; the temperature is 113 degrees Fahrenheit.

12. Spending the night at Abu Saeed's house.

13. The morning wake-up service: two American Apache helicopters above Abu Saeed's house.

14. Difficult return: a police patrol armored with machine guns closed down the street shortly after Ramadi.

15. Close-up of one of the patrol cars: the masked policeman stands behind a BKC machine gun.

There is a breathless silence in the room. Zaid is also staring in fascination at Abu Bassim. He had never seen a senior leader of the resistance in Anbar province before. I am astonished by the fact that Abu Saeed brought Zaid along to this meeting.

In an adjacent room, women, I never get to see have, prepared an evening meal of grilled carp—something I loved to eat on the banks of the Tigris in Baghdad before the war—and kebabs, grilled chicken, lots of vegetables and delicious honeydew and water melon.

As in almost all Muslim countries, people eat with their bare hands out of common bowls. Abu Saeed keeps picking out particularly fine pieces of fish or chicken for me and holds them up to my mouth with his right hand, as a brother would do. I really cannot warm to this way of being fed, so each time I ask Abu Saeed to put the morsels on my plate. I cover them discreetly with a piece of pita bread and hope nobody notices.

After the meal it is time for night prayers, and then the endless discussion resumes. I am asked what European governments think of the resistance. I do not know the answer; nor do the governments, I suspect. Abu Bassim tells me the resistance would like to establish contact with governments in Europe, to explore ways to create a just peace in Iraq. He says the high command of the nationalist resistance—which evidently knows about my visit—expressly requested that he convey this message.

I ask Abu Bassim, who is a Sunni, if, after the Americans pull out, he could accept a Shi'ite head of government and a cabinet and a parliament with two thirds of their members Shi'ites—which is quite likely given the structure of the population.

Abu Bassim looks perplexed. Are government positions and parliamentary seats assigned in the United States or Germany on the basis of religious denomination?

That is medieval nonsense. He says I am repeating almost verbatim the very argument of the Americans that led to the terrible chaos in Iraq in the first place.

I know that he is not altogether wrong, but I nevertheless ask again what would happen if, after the American troops are withdrawn, free elections led, for whatever reason, to a large Shi'ite majority?

"If a Shi'ite government is elected in an honorable, patriotic and free manner, then we shall of course accept it. Without a doubt." The men in the group nod their heads in agreement.

One problem with the current government, one of the men says, is that quite a high percentage of its members also have Iranian passports. "We do not want a pro-Iranian government," adds another. "And nor do the majority of Shi'ites in Iraq." [19]

For the first time this evening Abu Bassim laughs. As you probably know, he says to me, after the invasion the Americans published a set of 55 playing cards bearing the photos of the men on their most wanted list, the most powerful political and military leaders in Saddam Hussein's regime.

Thirty-six of the 55, about two thirds of the men, were Shi'ites. That is indisputable proof that the assertion that Iraq is divided along religious and confessional lines that have been at each others' throats since time immemorial is rubbish—invented as an attempt to break Iraq from within by those who have failed to conquer it from without.

I ask Abu Bassim what he thinks will happen when the Americans leave. He answers briefly and dryly: If the resistance and the people concentrate on fighting terrorism and on driving out the militias, that problem will soon be resolved. Ramadi is the proof.

We do not need the Americans to achieve that, Abu Bassim says. He cannot understand the West's arrogant argument that the Americans must stay in Iraq to prevent civil war. It is like saying that a sick physician who has brought the plague and cholera into a country must stay to combat the plague and cholera.

When the Americans are gone, Al-Qaeda looses its main enemy, and thus its main argument for being here. The few remaining Iraqi members would soon abandon their leaders. The same is true of the Shi'ite and Sunni militias. Most members are merely free-riders. It will not take long to deal with the rest. In Iraq, there is no "Hindu Kush" where the terrorists could hide.

In any case, the American government knowingly exaggerates the strength of Al-Qaeda. There have never been more than 3,000 foreign Al-Qaeda fighters in Iraq. The number now is more likely 2,000 or even lower. But Bush desperately needs Al-Qaeda in order to remain in Iraq. Al-Qaeda is his last remaining justification for the war. But within weeks of an American withdrawal, Al-Qaeda will simply vanish.

"The chaos came with the Americans, and it will go with the Americans. A swift withdrawal is only bad for the Americans. For the Iraqis it is good." [20]

The American withdrawal would take at least six months, Abu Bassim says with a smirk. "In that time we will rebuild our army and our police. They will be multi-confessional and multi-ethnic. And above all it will be successful."

Much of the military and government elite fled the country because of the Americans. Most of them will return when the U.S. troops are gone.

The reason why the United States is failing to establish an effective army and efficient police force is obvious: "The really good soldiers and police officers refuse to cooperate with the Americans. They are either not in the country or with the resistance."

"But what if, nevertheless, a civil war does erupt?" I ask. Abu Bassim looks at me very earnestly as he replies: "The chaos in Iraq cannot get any worse than it is now. But even if it were to, that is a matter for the Iraqis to deal with themselves, this is our country. We are a tribal society. Over the course of their long history, the Iraqi tribes have always succeeded in overcoming their differences. And they will continue to do so in the future."

It is past midnight when I take one of the foam mattresses Abu Bassim has provided and look for a quiet corner to sleep in his garden. The spot I choose is almost romantic—under a small orange tree, and surrounded by palm trees. These are not times to be too choosy about where to sleep.

I see that the other men have not gone to bed but are sitting in a corner of the garden; some are playing dominoes. I still do not know which of them is the leader of the resistance.

Abu Bassim's five-year-old grandson Abdullah has been allowed to stay up late. He is watching the game intently; for him it is no doubt much more interesting than our long conversations.

Return to Al-Jazeera

It was a wonderful night. I slept until eight o'clock in the morning. Abu Saeed tells me with a laugh that all attempts to wake me had failed. Almost everybody had tried shaking me, but I just slept on peacefully with a smile on my face. But now we definitely have to go. From now on, we shall have to spend every night in a different location. Word of my visit has got out.

I just have time to take a quick shower and brush my teeth, and we are off. This time we take a different route. After a short stop in Al-Sufia, where we take some photos, we suddenly arrive back at Abu Saeed's house at about 11 a.m.

I am surprised and ask why we have come back here, given that we had to leave in a hurry the day before. Abu Saeed smiles. Just as I did not expect us to return to Al-Jazeera, he explains, others will not either. Then he goes to greet his family and little Ali. They are no doubt another reason why he wanted to return home.

I go with Zaid into the reception room, which is dark even during the day. The gang of sassy children has gathered in unusual quietness in front of the television. They are watching with great attentiveness the arrival of the Iraqi national soccer team in Baghdad on Al Sharqiya, the commercial Iraqi station that broadcasts from Dubai.

The players have actually dared to spend 30 hours in the capital city of their native country—but only inside the Green Zone, the fortified compound in which the American military commanders and the Iraqi government have barricaded themselves. Some of the soccer stars, who are all under contract in other countries, have returned to Iraq for the first time in years.

Only carefully selected Iraqis are permitted to enter the Green Zone to cheer and wave at the team. But that does not worry the children of Abu Saeed and Abu Hamid. Their team has come home and is only 110 kilometers (68 miles) away. And that is just great news!

One of the boys starts a cushion fight, and all hell breaks loose as the children laugh and wallop each other. But they stop immediately when Akram, Abu Saeed's 18-year-old nephew, enters the room. He has got hold of his uncle's cell phone and now they can play games on it. The children crowd around Akram, who keeps glancing at the door, in case his uncle comes looking for his phone.

After half an hour, they loose interest in the phone and start to tell each other stories. They talk quietly, as Zaid has fallen asleep next to me. It is evidently time for a little siesta.

Outside it is 111 °F; here in the reception room it is nice and cool. Surprisingly enough, the air conditioning is working.

From where I am sitting, I look into the lobby, where a small gold-framed mirror, about 40 centimeters (16 in.) tall, is hanging on one of the walls. None of the boys passes the mirror without checking his looks and picking up the brush lying in front of the mirror to refresh his hairstyle—either pulling his hair back or brushing it forward.

Even Abu Hamid, who does not have much hair left on his head, smoothes it lovingly every time he passes the mirror. Who knows how long there will be any left to caress?

To the left of the mirror is the door leading to the private quarters of the families of Abu Saeed and Abu Hamid. That is where the women and girls usually spend the day. I notice that the women keep peeking round the door at me and whispering. It is not everyday that they get to see a doctor from Germany dozing in Ramadi.

I would love to know what they are saying. When they see that I am also observing them, they quickly disappear behind the door—only to take another peek just moments later.

Abu Saeed has joined me and offers some tea. I accept and thank him, turning away my eyes from his family's private quarters. I do not wish to offend him.

A few minutes later his wife Aisha comes and sits beside him. I ask Abu Saeed if I may take a photo of the two of them. He answers in a friendly but firm tone that that would be out of the question.

His wife has a different view of the matter. She gives me a quick smile, and in gentle loving tones tries to persuade her husband. It takes all of two minutes, and Abu Saeed gives in. It is clear who wears the pants in this family.

I take some pictures of the two of them. In the end they let me photograph Aisha together with their daughter Shahla. Then we look at the pictures on my digital camera. Aisha is very pleased. She utters a cheerful "shukran—thank you," and leaves the room.

While we were taking pictures, Zaid woke up. He enjoyed watching Aisha wind Abu Saeed around her little finger. "That is our fate," I quip, and Zaid nods in agreement.

I ask Zaid what his greatest dream is. "Peace," he replies. And then a large family, at least 12 children, "so there will be lots of action at home!" Just two or three children would be boring, he says. If God grants him and his wife children, he will name their two first sons Haroun and Karim after his brothers. Zaid falls silent. The memory of his slain brothers casts a shadow over his face.

After a while he starts to talk again: His wife should be well behaved and very pretty. It will be up to her whether to wear a headscarf, a hijab, but he would certainly prefer that. It is part of their religion, and religion is important. The Virgin Mary—he calls her Maryam—also wears a veil on the pictures he has seen. But he will not argue with his wife about the hijab and she will certainly not have to cover her entire body with a black abaya.

He could imagine marrying a Shi'ite or Kurdish woman. "But what about a foreigner?" I ask. Of course, Zaid answers, if he loves her and if she loves him, why not? "You Westerners ask funny questions." Zaid sounds almost offended.

"We have the same dreams as you. I would like to have a large family and a big Japanese car—your German cars are too expensive—and eventually, if I work hard and am successful, a little house of my own. I think you can achieve anything if you work hard."

Zaid's Resistance

To try to make these dreams come true, Zaid will have to wait a long time, and he knows it. There is a war raging in his country, his brothers are dead, and he is a resistance fighter. Any day could be his last, even if for the moment there is a ceasefire in downtown Ramadi. He could be asked to join an operation anywhere in the region tomorrow.

I ask him what he associates with the name "United States." When he was a child, he admired the United States because it was a land of progress and advancement—despite the harsh and painful sanctions imposed on Iraq. But the war has made him change his mind completely. That holds true for the entire Muslim world.

"We have never done anything to them, and still they have destroyed our country and our lives." He doubts he can ever forgive the Americans for the death of his brothers. He will never forget those hours as his little brother bled to death in front of his very eyes—never ever.

Then I ask the question Zaid most dreads—and that I dread most as well. I ask when he first took part in an attack on American troops. "Four months ago, in April 2007," he tells me after a long pause.

After Karim died, he decided to join a group made up of nationalists and Ba'athists. Each member has a specific task. One plans attacks, another explores possible sites, some are specialists in making roadside bombs, others in hiding them in the ground, and still others are experts in the use of RPGs—rocket propelled grenades.

He is responsible for remote detonations, Zaid tells me. He received a thorough training. He builds the detonators out of old cell phones and TV remote controls. It is not difficult. In effect, he decides whether a bomb goes off or not.

Zaid, Abu Saeed and I are now alone in the reception room.

Abu Saeed has sent all the others away. Abu Hamid is standing in front of the door to stop anyone entering the room. I ask Zaid if it did not terrify him to have the power to decide whether young American soldiers will live or die.

Zaid clenches his teeth. The American soldiers did not think twice before targeting and shooting his brothers, he retorts. He knows that many people in America are against this war, but they re-elected Bush despite his lies and despite the death of hundreds of thousands of Iraqis and of many American soldiers.

He knows that there are decent American soldiers in Ramadi. Many of them are also against the war. Once some American soldiers detained a young Iraqi and beat him up badly. An American officer intervened and took the Iraqi boy to his small office and cleaned, disinfected and dressed his wounds. He would like to meet this officer, when there is peace. But now it is war. He hopes nothing happens to this American.

The most important thing when launching an attack is to make sure that no civilians are harmed or killed, Zaid says. The life of civilians is sacred to him. Even if he could blow up the entire headquarters of the U.S. Army in Ramadi, he would not do it if that also meant killing just one civilian.

It is the greatest of crimes to kill civilians. "To kill an innocent person is worse than destroying the Ka'ba in Mecca a thousand times," he says. He has never injured or killed a civilian and will never do so, nor would he kill or harm civilians from other countries or of different faiths. The Qur'an explicitly forbids it.

This is a very important point for Zaid; it was the central issue for almost everyone I spoke to in Iraq. Zaid sets out his position with great clarity and seriousness. He is a resistance fighter and not a terrorist.

What he does, he says, is done in self defense, and therefore it is permissible. He will not wait until the Americans also murder his sisters and parents. Beyond a certain point, resistance is not just a right, but also a duty. This became clear to him with the death of his second brother. He must follow this road to the end now, until the Americans leave the country.

Zaid adds calmly: "You would not just stand by and watch if they shot your brothers or sisters in front of your very eyes. Nobody would, anywhere in the world."

In April 2007, Zaid and four other members of his group go one night to a spot they had earlier identified on Ishrin Street. Before morning prayers they dig a hole beside the road, place an explosive device in the hole and carefully fill it in again, and sprinkle sand over it.

The device was a *Nimsawiya* shell; Nimsawiya means "Austrian." This kind of shell was originally made for an Austrian-built gun. The replicas made in Iraq are about 60 centimeters (24 in.) long and seven and a half centimeters (3 in.) in diameter.

Zaid takes up position 100 meters (109 yards) away behind a wall. From here, he has a good view of the street and the spot where they buried the bomb. He waits for the military convoy that comes down Ishrin Street every morning.

The two hours Zaid has to wait seem like an eternity. Suddenly, at 7:30 a.m., he spots the first sand-colored Humvee in the distance.

He knows that in about one minute he will have to press the

button on the small remote detonation device that he himself had constructed.

It felt like slow motion, Zaid recalls, as the Humvees approached the spot. For a moment he sees before his mind's eye the faces of young helmeted American soldiers in their armored Humvees; they of course know they are driving down the most dangerous street in Ramadi; they are probably as scared as he is of dying at any moment in this mad war; perhaps they are joking, trying to encourage and cheer each other up.

But Zaid only thinks for that one moment about the American GIs; then he remembers Haroun and Karim lying in pools of blood. He remembers how his sisters and parents cried and held him back and how he pounded with his fists on the wall that separated him from his dying brother.

The Humvees are just a few meters from the spot where the bomb is to explode. Zaid's whole body is shaking. Because he has tears in his eyes, recalling about Haroun and Karim, he can only see the Humvees indistinctly. He knows the moment has come to detonate. He closes his eyes. But he cannot do it. "Press the button!" he tells himself. A thousand images race through his head.

Then he depresses the detonator. He does not see how the first two Humvees are hurled into the air, and how a huge cloud of black smoke rises above Ishrin Street, or how the fragments of the vehicles fall back to the ground as if in slow motion. He does hear the massive, dull thud of the blast.

Zaid runs away along the planned escape route, avoiding American and Iraqi checkpoints. He runs faster than he has ever run in his whole life, until he has left the city center. Then he tries to breathe deeply and walk at a normal pace.

When he reaches home, he goes into his bedroom, which he used to share with his two brothers and which is now his alone. His parents are already in their grocery store next door.

Zaid throws himself on his mattress and buries his face in a pillow. He tries to clear his mind and order his thoughts, but he fails. He keeps seeing those young American soldiers, hearing the sound of the explosion, and then seeing Haroun and Karim.

At about 10 o'clock his sisters tug gently at his shirt; with a gruff gesture he tells them to leave him alone. He lies there well into the afternoon. When his mother asks whether anything is wrong, he shakes his head and buries it again in his pillow.

He does not get up until evening, when he goes to meet the other members of his group. They are all there. Rashid, who had remained at his secure observation post after the explosion, reports that two Humvees were completely destroyed and that at least three American soldiers were killed, and several more injured.

After the blast more Humvees and several ambulances rushed to the scene. American soldiers stormed nearby houses and secured the area. As usual, they took away a number of sleepy young Iraqis who had had nothing to do with the blast. Then special vehicles came to carry away the wrecks of the Humvees. They cleaned up the area, trying to remove all traces of the attack.

Zaid listens to this report in silence. His friends want to congratulate him on his first military success, but he turns away and leaves. Zaid does not want to talk to anyone.

He goes down to the bank of the Euphrates, to the gentle elevation from which Karim liked to jump into the water. He sits there for hours, his head utterly empty. Now there is no escape and no way back: he has become part of this hateful war. He has known that since he saw Karim bleed to death.

Zaid's Bitterness

Zaid, Abu Saeed and I are sitting together in silence. I want to ask a thousand questions, but I see the sadness and bitterness in Zaid's eyes: He has so many reasons to be sad and bitter.

I know that there is one more question I have to ask Zaid—for my sake and for the sake of those who will read his story. I ask if he ever thinks of the parents of the young American soldiers he has killed. Those parents and even those sons might also have been against this war, just as he is.

Zaid looks at me long and hard, and answers with another question: "Have these people ever thought about my family, even for a moment? Do American families, does anybody in the West ever think of the countless Iraqi families that have lost children, brothers, sisters, or parents?

"Why should I think about the families of the soldiers who murdered my brothers? I cannot do that, and I do not want to. They have destroyed our country with their tanks, and they have ruined the lives of my family. They have no right or reason to be here."

Zaid stands up and leaves the room. Abu Saeed and I look at each other in silence. His little son Ali comes in with his half-deflated football. He wants to play with me. But playing is the last thing I can do at this very moment.

Aisha

Suddenly Abu Saeed's wife Aisha is standing next to us. She saw Zaid leave the room, deathly pale and overwrought. She evidently heard some of the conversation. She talks to me in her wonderful gentle voice. Abu Saeed does not translate what she says, but tells her that our discussion with Zaid was nothing for women.

In kind but firm tones, Aisha tells Abu Saeed that he is wrong and asks him to translate what she has to say. As usual, Abu Saeed backs down, and starts to translate her words.

Of course women are deeply concerned about this war, Aisha tells me. After all, they are the mothers of the resistance fighters. "Zaid's mother Amira and I are good friends. As you know, I also have five children. We talk about our families. Amira often cries about Haroun and Karim, the two sons she has lost; and she is frightened for Zaid, the only son she has left. She thinks they might shoot him too one day, just like they shot his brothers."

She also fears that Zaid might break apart inside; after Karim's death, he hardly ate or spoke for weeks and weeks. He is like a different person—melancholic and withdrawn. He used to be such a happy boy; now he hardly ever laughs. At night, he has nightmares and often wakes up screaming and drenched in sweat.

"Zaid may look like a man," Aisha continues, "but in reality he is still a child, and he cannot cope with the loss of his brothers, with fighting in the resistance, and with the suffering of the people of Ramadi. Zaid has known nothing but war and hardship his entire life—the war with Iran until 1988, then the Gulf War in 1991, the economic sanctions and now, since 2003, this war.[21]

He has seen so many people die, adults and children, because of the war and hunger. He has enjoyed so few carefree moments in his life.

"My little boy Ali, who is four, also knows nothing but war. What will become of him? What if his father, or his brothers and sisters are killed one day by the Americans? Everybody knows that the war will continue in Anbar. Will Ali run away? Will he become a resistance fighter? What should I tell him if he says he wants to join the fight? Should I say it would be futile? What should we mothers tell our children?

"Can you not make your American friends understand that they have to stop presenting our children with this horrible alternative—either to stand by and watch their families being slaughtered or to kill someone themselves? Tell them to end this war, which is killing both their young soldiers and our sons—for no reason at all.

We cannot take it anymore. There is hardly a mother in Iraq who is not weeping for her sons, her children. What did we ever do to the Americans?"

Aisha has become pale. Abu Saeed takes her in his arms. "I am not reproaching you," Aisha adds quietly, "perhaps you can help. There must be mothers in your country and in America who understand the mothers of Iraq." Aisha leaves the room in tears.

I need some time to reflect on what Aisha has said, as does Abu Saeed. In silence, we go out into the garden. The boys have started to eat supper. Who knows when they will again enjoy such delicious food.

After supper the men say their night prayers. This time I

join them and pray with them—but I say my own prayer. "Allahu Akbar—God is greater."

If there is a God, and I firmly believe there is, then he certainly does not distinguish between Muslims, Jews and Christians. I ask Allah-Yahveh-God to help the people of Iraq and to grant them peace. I give thanks that we in the West may live in peace. I really do not know what we did to deserve it. Allahu Akbar!

At one in the morning I lie down on my mattress. I know I shall not sleep well tonight. I shall think of Zaid's brothers Haroun and Karim, but also of the day in April 2007 when Zaid took part in his first attack. I shall think of the many American soldiers who have died in Ramadi and are yet to die in Ramadi, and of the much greater number of Iraqi civilians who have been killed by American soldiers, by Al-Qaeda, and by the death squads of power-hungry politicians—and of those who are yet to be killed; and I shall think of the many wounded, maimed and crippled on both sides.

I am very tired, but also very agitated and tense. I am startled by every noise from the street beyond the garden gate.

I have not felt this way since my visits to Afghanistan in the 1980s, when Soviet helicopters circled above us and we had to take cover in ditches or under trees. It also reminded me of Algiers in 1960, when I spent a few days with an Arab family there during the Algerian war of liberation. The sound of a car stopping outside, or loud voices, would scare us up and we'd listen closely.

The atmosphere on this night is uncanny, even unnerving. Helicopters fly low over the house again and again as though they are looking for something directly nearby. It takes me a long time to fall asleep. I dream horrible dreams and keep waking up.

It is not yet dawn when Abu Saeed comes to me and says: "We have to leave immediately. Certain groups have decided to pay us a visit today. There are all kinds of wild rumors circulating about you. Too many people have seen you, and the children have been proudly telling the other children in the neighborhood about the stranger staying with them who speaks English.

"People in Ramadi have not seen a Westerner without an American escort in years. And there are probably a few foreign Al-Qaeda terrorists here as well. You have to get out at once. Changing locations is not good enough any longer."

Still half asleep, I mumble something about the two more days I am meant to spend in Ramadi. I tell Abu Saeed that I have only seen snapshots so far; I need to spend much more time here if I am really to understand everything.

But Abu Saeed is adamant. The situation is critical. The Americans, Abu Saeed says, have stepped up their patrols because there has been heavy fighting again here in Anbar province. A Chinook helicopter has been shot down between Fallujah and Ramadi, and near Rutba an American patrol hit a mine as it crossed a bridge over the highway. The vehicle was destroyed and the bridge seriously damaged. U.S. forces across Anbar are on high alert.

While I am still battling sleep, Abu Saeed has a heated conversation on his cell phone. He yells something like "Almani," which means German. I hear the words "Al-Qaeda" and "raids" several times. Then Abu Saeed says he is very sorry, but he can no longer take responsibility for my safety.

In a daze, I collect my belongings. Exposing my hosts to mortal danger or being seized by the Americans during a raid in

Anbar province would not be a good idea. Abu Saeed is right. Nonetheless, I would very much like to stay longer. I still want answers to a thousand questions I have about Iraq.

Abu Saeed repeats in a gruff voice: "We have to go. Immediately. One hour from now, we will not be able to get away. They are sealing the area." I go straight to the car. This morning there is no coffee waiting for me.

Moussa has started the engine. Abu Saeed is already in the car. This time, his family is staying at home. Abu Saeed has not had time to organize the departure of his family as well.

As I am about to get in, Zaid appears before me. "I would like to visit you in Germany, when the war is over. May I?" he asks quietly.

"Perhaps," I answer. I feel very bad about leaving while these people have to be left behind in all their misery. "Call me if you or your family have any problems because of me. I shall try to help you. I promise." Zaid turns away silently.

I shall never forget this young man, no matter what, or the many tears shed by the people I have met in Ramadi. This damned dishonorable fraudulent war, in which there are only losers.

It makes me sick to think that some people in the West still dream and talk of "victory" in Iraq. I feel ashamed of the indifference with which we in the West watch the Iraqi tragedy unfold. I have rarely experienced such deep shame as I have during these days in Ramadi.

I slam the car door shut and look one last time over at Abu Saeed's family sleeping peacefully on the lawn, wrapped in blankets. Then we set off, with Moussa driving as fast as the bumpy road permits.

Return to Syria

As always, Moussa takes a number of detours to avoid as many checkpoints as possible. It takes half an hour to get out of Al-Jazeera and onto the highway to Damascus. I notice that in the early-morning rush I put on Abu Saeed's sandals. I must have left my sneakers—and who knows what else—at his house.

I am about to curse myself for my clumsiness, when Moussa suddenly brakes hard. We are just outside Ramadi; three white-and-blue police pickup trucks overtake. Standing on the bed of each truck are one or two masked Iraqi police officers behind a machine gun. The pickup trucks pass us slowly. The masked men peer in through our tinted windows in the pre-dawn gloom. Their machine guns are directed at us.

Though I fear trouble is brewing, I get out my camera. Poor Abu Saeed explodes in rage, and I put it down next to my seat. The tension in the SUV is almost palpable. Moussa, our usually silent driver, also asks me not to take any photos. I nod and pat him on the shoulder. I do not want him to lose his nerve.

Moussa has brought our Chevrolet to a halt, to try to maintain the required 150 meters distance to the police pickups in front of us. But the sinister trucks with their masked gunners stop just 50 meters ahead.

Ahead is a large junction. We have no idea what is going on. All we know is that the heavily armed police officers on the pickups have the same rights as American soldiers. That means, they may shoot at once, if for any reason they feel they are under threat.

At the crossroads, about 200 meters ahead, four more pickups appear on the left and the right. On each, frowning figures man a machine gun. And just beyond the junction, coming the other way, two more heavily-armed flatbed trucks take up position. A total of nine pickups are now blocking the highway.

The one immediately in front of us, about 50 meters away, suddenly backs up, its machine gun still pointing our way. My blood freezes in my veins. The pickup stops again just a few meters from our SUV. One of the masked officers yells and waves his arm at us.

Abu Saeed, who is looking very pale, barks at Moussa: "Back up! Fast!" Moussa slams the car into reverse and floors the gas pedal, putting at least 200 meters between us and them—just to be on the safe side. I think to myself it would be very nice if the machine gun was pointing in a different direction.

Minutes pass. Suddenly we see in the distance beyond the junction a military convoy coming towards us. So that must be the reason why these nine pickups mounted with machine guns are here to secure the crossroads. We all breathe a sigh of relief

Abu Saeed angrily lectures Moussa, telling him that he always has to stop when an armed pickup passes. Especially since an American patrol was blown up on a bridge over this very highway only yesterday. He scolds me as well: I should pack away my damned camera!

We are all as white as a sheet—and not just because of a lack of sleep.

The military supply convoy passes. After half an hour we can resume our journey. Moussa floors it, this time in a forward direction. He turns off the air conditioning, explaining that at high speed and with such poor-quality gas the engine would otherwise overheat. It seems as if Moussa wants to get out of his own country as fast as he can.

We still have 450 kilometers (280 miles) to go. The mood in the Chevrolet is still unbearably tense. Bathed in sweat, I stare out of the window into the Iraqi desert littered with burned-out wrecks. How many Iraqis and how many Americans have died on this highway?

Moussa again plays his cassette of fiery sermons; Abu Saeed dozes; and I write notes and I empty my first of many bottles of water.

After five and a half hours, at midday, we reach the Iraqi border fortifications. Among the wrecks, a sign in Arabic thanks us for visiting Iraq—shukran liziaratikum. "You're welcome," I think. But I will not be coming back any time soon, at least not until the situation changes.

Beyond the first set of checkpoints we again pass through the five-kilometer stretch of no man's land, between high walls, passing by the Palestinian refugees and their tents.

All the misery of the world is to be found here in such a concentrated form. What will the children growing up in these dirty tents think, when they are adults, of those who drove them out into this place, and of those who would not let them in, and of those who caused this entire catastrophe?

After a few minutes, we see another sign: "Ahlan wasaha lan bikom fi Soria—welcome to Syria."

I feel such immense relief. I am out again; it is over. No more armored Humvees, American armored personnel carriers, reconnaissance helicopters, or F-16 fighter jets. No more masked Iraqi police officers! No more fear of crazed Christian GIs or crazed Muslim suicide bombers. No more "ceasefire" in a four-kilometer zone around which bomb blasts hurl cars into the air and helicopters are shot out of the sky. What a sense of relief!

Although I could not admit this to myself either before or during my trip, I now acknowledge that Iraq filled me with fear, real visceral fear—for the first time in my life. I spent five days in this tormented country, five very long days. I never would have thought that I could feel such infinite relief upon entering Syria, of all places.

The Syrian border controls are even stricter for those entering from Iraq than for those leaving Syria. We have to see the head of the border police, an elegant officer of about 40. He thinks Abu Saeed is joking when he says that I am a physician and had been to Ramadi to assess first hand the situation of the people living there. "No German would go there," he retorted with a smile. "No foreigner ever goes there, at least not without an armored car and armed guard."

When Abu Saeed mentions the ceasefire, the officer cuts him short with a hearty laugh. "Ceasefire? In Anbar province? With how many killed every night? Ten instead of 20? Do you know how many people are killed on the highway between here and Ramadi every week? There were more roadside bomb attacks in July than in any month since the war began!"

Abu Saeed argues passionately. I think he fears the border guards might send me back to Iraq. The officer, who has the suave good looks of a movie star, still does not believe a word he says.

But I really do not look very dangerous or suspicious. Eventually he gives us back our passports and says we may go. Then he picks up his phone.

We go back to our car, where another border official is waiting for us. Apparently the officer had just called him. Unfortunately, he tells us, we have to go to the head of customs. Abu Saeed seems to have an inkling of what is going on.

But this junior official will not be deterred by an offer of baksheesh from taking us to the customs post. Abu Saeed's brow is distinctly furrowed. "He is taking us to the head of intelligence. Stick to your story about being a physician, otherwise things could get nasty."

Abu Saeed was right. We are escorted into the small office of the top man here. He is wearing a sleeveless undershirt. He is about 35 years of age and he has a receding hairline of dark brown hair. He looks almost European. Abu Saeed tells him that I am a physician and shows him my invitation from the Iraqi interior ministry and our passports; Abu Saeed talks and talks. But the intelligence guy just laughs.

He does not believe Abu Saeed either. "A German in August in Anbar province?" He has never heard such a silly story. Still, he cannot send us back, and after a while he returns our passports to us.

He has a small request, he adds. One of his men has a bad sore throat. And since I am here, could I not take a look?

My heart sinks—I have been called out! I gather my wits and decide the best policy will be to say the man must be taken to the hospital immediately, if he really does look sick.

We are taken to another small room, which is both very hot and very drafty. A heavyset Syrian of about 25 with a shaved head enters and points to his throat. I point to his mouth and tell him to open it. He obeys and opens it as wide as it goes. I depress his tongue with a small ruler. His throat is inflamed and covered by white spots. It looks like a straightforward case of strep throat.

I remember my mother's old remedy for sore throats. "Gargle with sea salt every two hours," I tell him. Abu Saeed translates the diagnosis and the prescribed treatment. The official looks at me aghast: "Gargle with what? We do not have any sea salt here."

"If you cannot get any sea salt at the pharmacy," I tell him, "dissolve an aspirin in water and gargle with it before you go to bed. Gargle for a long time, then swallow. That even helps against gingivitis."

The official nods gratefully, even though he does not have gingivitis. My final word of advice is: "And shut the door! Your office is so drafty, anyone would get sick."

The fat Syrian hugs me in gratitude as he says shukran—thank you! Meanwhile, I am thanking my mother in heaven for having had a trusty remedy for all my childhood ailments. "Yallah!" says Abu Saeed, indicating we need to move on. He seems to regret having sold my doctorate in law as a doctorate in medicine.

Hanan

With a renewed sense of relief, we drive on towards Damascus. Nobody is feeling talkative now. Moussa has been rather sullen all along. I ask him why he never says anything. He looks straight ahead at the road and remains silent. After a while, he says quietly: "I used to like talking about my life, back then when I was a driver for the police in Baghdad. Then the war came, and all the misery. If I start to talk, it all wells up again."

"I had an aunt in Baghdad, her name was Hanan," Moussa tells me. "Her husband died young. She was of small body height but very beautiful. She never remarried, and mourned his death for many years. Eventually she decided to find new meaning in her life. From that day on, she supported the large families of her two younger brothers Salim and Jamil.

"Every morning at six o'clock she got to work washing, ironing and cooking for Salim's family of nine. Everything had to be spotless and tidy. Then in the afternoon she went to Jamil's house, to do the same for his family of twelve. She worked non-stop, and hardly ever took a break. Nothing was too much for her.

"But over the years the hard work wore her down. Her skin became wrinkly and tanned, and she looked like the old women at the market who sell fruit and vegetables. But she was always so full of love that everybody loved her too.

"All she cared about was to help the wives of her brothers and to help make their families happy. In the evenings she would read to the children, and later the grandchildren, or tell them stories of her childhood. She was very happy, because she had not one, but two families.

"One day in fall 2006, Hanan was out shopping for her two families—she was already over 60 and a little frail—when suddenly fighting erupted between Americans and resistance fighters nearby.

"The U.S. soldiers must have called in the helicopters, which then bombed the neighborhood where Hanan's two brothers lived. "Hanan heard the bombs explode and saw the clouds of smoke, and hurried home as fast as she could. Her bags were heavy, as she had such large families to feed.

"She was already out of breath as she turned into the small road where her brother Salim and his family lived. She saw at once that his house had been completely destroyed. She dropped her bags and ran, screaming, to the site. Neighbors were standing in front of the rubble, distraught and angry.

"Hanan cried out: 'Where is Salim? Where is Zainab? Where are my children?' The neighbors just pointed to the smoking ruins, or turned away in tears.

"My frail aged aunt threw herself on the rubble and tried with her bare hands to remove the stones one by one, to dig a hole through the rubble. She wept and cried, and blood poured from her hands. She lay down on the rubble that had buried her beloved children and grandchildren and family. She covered her head in ashes. She wanted to die, just as her family had died.

"After an hour, she got up, collected her bags of shopping, and sat down on a low wall opposite the ruins of the house. She pulled her black veil low over her eyes. She sat there crying and groaning until the evening.

"The neighbors invited her into their homes and to eat with them. But they could not persuade her and gave up. Hanan just wanted to stay there, close to her children, her grandchildren, her family. Somebody had brought her a bottle of water, but she did not touch it.

"At sundown, the neighborhood imam came to her and asked where she would spend the night. 'At Jamil's house,' she replied in a faint whisper. The imam tried to talk with her, but he could not find the words. He turned away helplessly and left, wiping the tears from his eyes. He took a deep breath, clenched his fists, and went back to Hanan. He tried to remain calm as he said: 'You cannot go to Jamil's house, because it too has been destroyed. They are all dead.'

"Hanan, this little old woman bent over in agony, raised herself, slowly pulled her veil up from her eyes and stared at the imam in disbelief. She scrutinized his face as if it might confirm that she had misheard his words. She shook her head in despair: 'No, that cannot be true. It is impossible.

'Tell me it is not so,' she implored. 'Jamil is alive, and I shall go to him, as always. And nobody will stop me.' 'You cannot go to Jamil,' the imam replied softly. 'He is no longer there. They are all dead.'

"With a deep cry, Hanan threw herself on the ground, and clawed at the earth, and beat her fists on the road. She rested her head in the dust and wept. She lay there quite still.

"After an hour or so, the imam and some friends carried her to his house. The imam's wife brushed the dust out of her abaya and tried to clean her face and hands. She brought Hanan something to eat, but Hanan did not touch it. She just sat there sobbing and whimpering.

"Late in the evening relatives came and asked her to come back with them. We also asked her to come to our house—my family and I. Hanan did not respond. She had crumbled, collapsed in upon herself. She remained with the imam's family. She did not eat and she did not drink. She only cried.

"Three days later she died. She simply stopped breathing. She could not bear it any longer, and she did not want to carry on."

Moussa is holding the steering wheel very tight and is staring straight ahead. His eyes are dry. "Thousands of families in Iraq could tell you such stories, including people you met in Ramadi. They only told you a small part of what they have been through.

"Tell your American friends that they have not only destroyed our country but also broken our hearts." Moussa pauses for a moment. Then he adds quietly: "Hanan was Zaid's favorite aunt."

The outline of Damascus appears in the distance. Moussa and Abu Saeed will spend the night in Damascus and head back to Ramadi in the morning—to a country where most of the people have lost everything, including hope.

10:1

Our Horizon is not the End of the World: A Very Personal Afterword

Why do you see the speck in your neighbor's eye, but do not notice the log in your own eye?

NEW TESTAMENT, LUKE 6:41

While working on this book I took many trips and read a great deal.[1] I had only intended to read the two bestsellers by the French terrorism expert Gilles Kepel, *Jihad: The Trail of Political Islam* and *The War for Muslim Minds: Islam and the West.* They were to bring me up to date on the debate about terrorism. But the more I read, the more I realized how little I knew.

So I carried on reading. More and more. Devastating works such as *Coloniser, Exterminer* by Olivier Le Cour Grandmaison[2] and *L'Honneur de Saint-Arnaud* by François Maspero.[3] I met some of the authors I read: Le Cour Grandmaison, for example, a charming youthful French academic. When I was a student, I saw Jean-Paul Sartre, who wrote the preface to Frantz Fanon's classic *Wretched of the Earth*, in Paris in 1960.

I soon discovered that in order to understand the conflict between the West and the Muslim world I would have to read the Qur'an and the Old and New Testaments in their entirety and in relation to each other.

I used every free minute I had—in cars, on planes, on holiday, even in the fitness studio. I read much of the Qur'an while on an exercise bicycle, viewed with suspicion by those around me. They probably thought I was crazy. How on earth can one read the Qur'an in a fitness studio?

The most important lesson I learned from my reading and my travels was that the current debate about combating terrorism misses the point entirely. To focus on "the war on terror" or specific measures such as online searches, electronic tagging of "Islamists" or the monitoring of converts to Islam, means failure to appreciate the true dimensions of the problem.

We shall only overcome terrorism if we remove its causes, instead of trying to treat the symptoms. The main cause of terrorism nowadays is the inhuman way in which the West has dealt with the Muslim world over the past two centuries.[4] One may not continually humiliate peoples. Only when we treat Muslim countries as fairly as we wish to be treated ourselves, will we overcome terrorism.

I have summed up what I learned during my readings and 50 years of travels in this afterword. They are not scholarly theses; they represent my personal view of things. I have merely attempted to consider the events of the past two hundred years in the Middle East also from the perspective of a Muslim, and not only from that of a Westerner.

When I started my research, I looked hard for a commonly accepted definition of the phenomenon of terrorism. I discovered that there is none. The United Nations has been trying in vain for decades to find some consensus on the definition of the term. The same is true for the concepts of "resistance" and "war of liberation." One man's freedom or resistance fighter is another man's terrorist.[5]

Edward Peck, who was deputy director of the White House task force on terrorism under Ronald Reagan, highlighted how hard it was to come up with a useful definition with this sarcastic comment: "We produced about six, and in each and every case, they were rejected, because careful reading would indicate that our own country had been involved in some of those activities."[6]

I have adopted a very personal definition. It served as a point of orientation throughout my career in politics. For me, terrorism is the unacceptable attempt to attain political goals by means of killing or mistreating innocent civilians. Whoever kills or harms innocent civilians in order to impose his view of the world is, in my opinion, a terrorist—even if he is a head of state. We do not have the right to apply double standards when we judge injustice.

My theses are brief and condensed. They contain a wealth of historical facts, without which it is hard to understand the conflict between the Occident and the Orient—let alone solve it. They also include generalizations, which I readily concede are problematic. When I talk about "the West," I mean above all the political leadership of the major Western nations. There are Western countries that have not been guilty of colonialism or neo-colonialism. And there have been and are countless people in the West who passionately and unceasingly call for the fair treatment of Muslims.

The term "Muslim world" is also a generalization, which does not ultimately do justice to the diversity of Muslim societies. Nonetheless I find the term useful as I attempt to delineate in broad strokes and in comprehensible form the relationships between East and West. Despite all the differences between the various countries, it cannot—unfortunately—be denied that there is indeed a profound conflict between the "West" and the "Muslim world."

My theses will no doubt meet with much criticism. I accept that. I hope that a lot will be clarified in discussion. It is time for us to open our eyes. Our current policies towards the Muslim world have no future.

I.

The West is much more violent than the Muslim world. Millions of Muslim civilians have been killed since colonialism began.[7]

The great French historian and politician Alexis de Tocqueville[8] was a passionate champion of the freedom of the individual. For him, it always took precedence over equality. Inequality, he wrote, comes "directly from God."[9] So it is no wonder that, like most of his contemporaries, this enlightened statesman did not think highly of racial equality.

In his major work *Democracy in America*, published in 1835, Tocqueville made a remark that characterized the era: "If we reasoned from what passes in the world, we should almost say that the European is to the other races of mankind, what man is to the lower animals;—he makes them subservient to his use; and when he cannot subdue, he destroys them."[10] For the liberal thinker there was "consequently no reason to treat Muslim subjects as if they were equal to us."[11]

And that is precisely how the West has treated the Muslim world for the past 200 years. During the colonial period in Algeria for example, Muslim families were hunted like "hyenas, jackals and mangy foxes."[12] The strategy that the 19th-century colonial rulers adopted to break resistance to their "civilizing mission"[13] was to "ruin, hunt, terrorize" (Olivier Le Cour Grandmaison).[14] In Algeria entire tribes that had sought refuge in caves were "smoked out" (*enfumades*).[15]

The French colonel Lucien-François de Montagnac[16] wrote in a letter from Algeria in 1842: "We kill, we strangle. The cries of the desperate and dying mingle with the noise of the bellowing, bleating livestock. You ask me what we do with the women. Well, we keep some as hostages, others we exchange for horses, the rest are auctioned like cattle …[17] In order to banish the thoughts that sometimes besiege me, I have some heads cut off, not the heads of artichokes but the heads of men."[18]

Louis de Baudicour, a French writer and settler in Algeria,[19] described one of the many massacres: "A soldier cut off a woman's breast in jest, another grabbed a child by its legs and smashed its skull against a wall."[20] Victor Hugo reported that soldiers would throw children to each other in order to catch them on the tips of their bayonets.[21] They would get 100 sous for ears preserved in brine. The bonus for a severed head was higher. The bodies of Arabs were turned into animal charcoal (Oliver Le Cour Grandmaison).[22]

Napoleon III nonetheless saw the hand of God at work: "France is the mistress of Algeria because that is what God wanted."[23] Algerians saw it differently. They had to pay a very high price for their freedom. In the war of independence from 1954 to 1962, 8,000 Algerian villages were destroyed with napalm bombs by the French air force.[24]

The Algerian National Liberation Front (FLN)[25] also committed gruesome acts of terror, as Albert Camus rightly pointed out.[26] But in terms of numbers, there is no comparison between those acts and the violent deeds committed by the colonialists. During their 130-year "civilizing mission" they killed well over two million Algerians, according to Algerian sources. French estimates say more than one million Algerians and 100,000 French nationals were killed.[27]

The Iraqis, colonized by Britain, did not fare much better. When they rose up against British oppression in 1920, Winston Churchill accused them of "ingratitude"[28] and used chemical weapons against them—"with excellent moral effect," as he noted.[29]

"Bomber Harris," the spiritual father of "moral bombing," reported proudly after a bombing raid: "The Arabs and Kurds now know what real bombing means. Within 45 minutes an entire village can be practically wiped out."[30] In Iraq, bombing raids were also considered an effective way to persuade people to pay their taxes.[31] One Royal Air Force officer, Lionel Charlton,[32] resigned in 1924 after he visited a hospital and saw the mutilated victims of such a raid.[33] He could not know that his country would again bomb Iraq 80 years later.

In Libya, the colonial power Italy dropped phosgene and mustard gas on both rebels and civilians. Tribal leaders were taken up in airplanes and thrown out. More than 100,000 civilians were deported to camps in the desert; half of them perished. Libyan girls were kept as sex slaves for the colonial troops.[34] During the Kabyle rebellions in Morocco, Spain also used chemical weapons—to equally horrible effect.

The model for the treatment of the Arabs was the strategy adopted to wipe out the indigenous peoples of America.[35] The mad ideas about racial and cultural superiority prevalent at the time knew no bounds. Gustave Le Bon, founder of mass psychology and opponent of the "superstition of equality,"[36] divided mankind into four classes: the native Australian and American peoples he termed "primitive races": "Negroes" he classed as "inferior," Arabs and Chinese as "intermediate," and the Indo-Europeans as a "superior race."[37]

Since the Second World War, the West has often treated Muslims as subhuman beings on a "level with the superior apes" (Jean-Paul Sartre).[38] This is true of the wars against the colonial powers, interventions to secure supplies of raw materials, the question of Palestine, and the sanctions against Iraq, which were pushed through by the United States and Britain. According to UNICEF, these punitive measures against Iraq, which the Vatican called "perverse,"[39] caused the deaths of more than 1.5 million civilians, including half a million children.[40]

The current Iraq war also shows a breathtaking contempt for the Muslim world. Thousands of civilians were killed as U.S.-led forces marched in. Countless numbers were crippled by bombs, some of which contained uranium.[41] A study conducted by independent American and Iraqi physicians and published in the medical journal *The Lancet* estimates that more than 600,000 Iraqis had met with violent deaths by June 2006 as a result of the war and the chaos caused by occupation forces.

It says 31 percent were killed by U.S.-led coalition forces, and 24 percent as a result of sectarian violence and suicide attacks. Responsibility could not be attributed in 45 percent of the violent deaths; according to *The Lancet*, the high number of gunshot victims also suggests a "direct involvement of the U.S. military."[42]

A study by the independent British research institute ORB in January 2008 estimates that until then more than one million Iraqis had been killed and around the same number injured. It reports that in Baghdad almost one in two households has lost a family member.[43] According to Human Rights Watch, Saddam Hussein was responsible for the death of 290,000 Iraqi civilians in the course of his 23-year rule.[44]

Since fall 2007, the number of fatalities has declined in Iraq. But according to experts' conservative estimates, in the summer of 2008 more than 3,000 Iraqi civilians were still dying each month in the chaos of the war. That is as many as perished in the World Trade Center on September 11, 2001.

The people of Iraq are worse off now than they were under Saddam (according to Kofi Annan). There will not be many Iraqis who say: "Great, our country has been destroyed; more than a million people have been killed; four and a half million have been made refugees; the child mortality rate is one of the highest in the world; electricity, water and medicine are scarce; unemployment and inflation have risen to 50 percent; one can hardly go out onto the street;[45] in Baghdad people are living in walled ghettos, since 'good fences make good neighbors,' as General David Petraeus[46] put it—but it was worth it, Saddam is gone." The only beneficiaries of this disaster are Iran and radical Islamism.

Does it come as a surprise, then, that according to a survey conducted by the BBC and ABC, 86 percent of all Iraqis, no matter whether Shi'ites or Sunnis, demand the withdrawal of American troops? [47]

Over the past 200 years no Muslim state has ever attacked the West. European powers and the United States have always been the aggressors and not those under attack.[48] Since the beginning of the colonial era, millions of Muslim civilians have been killed. When it comes to killing, the West is leading by a ratio of more than ten to one. The current debate about the Muslim world's alleged propensity to violence is a mockery of the historical facts. The West was and is much more violent than the Muslim world. The problem of our era is not the violence of Muslims but the violence of some Western countries.

II.

In view of the warmongering of the West, it is not surprising that support for Muslim extremists continues to grow.

To understand Muslim extremism, one also has to try to see the world from the point of view of a Muslim. Our horizon is not the end of the world. A young Muslim who follows the news on television sees day after day how Muslim women, children and men are killed by Western weapons, Western allies and Western soldiers in Iraq, Afghanistan, Palestine, Lebanon, Somalia, and elsewhere.

It is cynical of great Western thinkers to furrow their brows and ponder the decline and fall of Arab civilization, which once was "militarily, economically and culturally far superior" (Hans Magnus Enzensberger).[49] The West played a major part in making that happen. It plundered and ravaged the colonies and then withdrew.

In 1830, when the colonization of Algeria began, it had a literacy rate of 40 percent, higher than that of France or England.[50] In 1962, when the French occupying forces pulled out, it was under 20 percent.[51] Colonialism stole from the Arab world more than a century of development. Seventeen years after the French conquest of Algeria, Tocqueville noted with resignation: "The lights have been extinguished ... We have made Muslim society much more miserable, disorganized, ignorant and barbaric."[52]

Western colonialism raged in almost all parts of the world. But in the oil-rich countries of the Middle East it never stopped. That sets the region apart and makes it a breeding ground for terrorism.

Terrorism is not a Muslim problem but a global one. It has always existed and has been used by all kinds of movements. Alongside Arab terrorists who murdered Jewish settlers, there were also "Zionist terrorist organizations" such as Irgun, led by Menachem Begin, and the Fighters for the Freedom of Israel, led by Itzhak Shamir, who described themselves as terrorists.[53] They used terrorist tactics—also against civilians—to fight the

British and the Arabs for a free Israel.[54]

In the current debate on terrorism it is often said: "Not all Muslims are terrorists, but all terrorists are Muslims."[55] That is simply wrong. Until September 11, 2001, the Hindu Tamil Tigers in Sri Lanka were considered the world's deadliest terrorist organization.[56] In their fight for freedom and independence, they professionalized and perfected suicide terrorism; and they were copied down to the last detail by others around the world, especially in the Middle East. They continue to bomb and to be bombed even today. But they do not kill Westerners. That is why their attacks are not reported in depth.

Of the 48 organizations classified as terrorist by the European Union in 2006,[57] 36 have nothing to do with Islam. These "anti-imperialist" or "anti-capitalist" terrorist groups are responsible for the deaths of countless civilians in Latin America, Asia and sub-Saharan Africa. In the West, they do not figure in public awareness because they do not kill people like us.

After the official end of colonial rule in the Middle East, the colonial powers were often replaced by financially and militarily dependent puppet regimes, pawns in the geopolitical game of Western great powers.

Whoever did not play along was advised that a people only has a right to self-determination as long as it does not infringe Western interests. Freedom never meant freedom from us. One might call this "lex Mossadeq" in memory of the Iranian prime minister Mohammad Mossadeq,[58] who was democratically elected in 1951 and deposed two years later by the CIA and the British Secret Intelligence Service (MI6).

Whoever fails to act in accordance with this law is ousted in a putsch or subjected to a concerted media campaign and branded a "rogue."[59] Using the media to create "villains" is a specialty of Western foreign policy. As the example of Gaddafi shows, the title of "rogue" can be revoked at any moment.

Even Saddam Hussein, a former "partner" who was renamed a "rogue," might still be doing as he pleases even today, had he remained a partner of the United States. The massacre of Dujail[60] in which 148 people died, and for which Saddam was later executed by the U.S., occurred in 1982. At the time Saddam was, for the United States, an important player in the Middle East and waged war with Western support against Khomeini's Iran. Donald Rumsfeld visited Saddam in 1983 as special envoy of the U.S. president, even though he had been thoroughly informed about Dujail.[61]

Saddam was, after all, our anti-Islamist comrade-in-arms: he was supplied by Germany with components for chemical weapons, by France with fighter jets, and by the United States with satellite data on Iranian positions.[62] In the Middle East, the West never showed real interest in human rights or democracy; it was and is fighting for oil.

Cynical dehumanization in the name of human rights, which the bloody images from Iraq, Afghanistan and other Muslim countries document daily, has left a deep and painful mark on the Muslims' cultural memory. Samuel Huntington was right on at least one point: "The West won the world not by the superiority of its ideas or values or religion, but rather by its superiority in applying organized violence. Westerners often forget this fact; non-Westerners never do."[63]

How can the Muslim world believe in our values of human dignity, the rule of law and democracy if all it sees is the way we oppress, humiliate and exploit it? Is it really surprising that extremists gain more and more support? Or that some people eventually hit back when their families are again and again mowed down by our machinery of destruction? Nobody is born a terrorist.

Despite all this, the kindness and hospitality still shown to Western visitors in Middle Eastern countries are overwhelming. One can visit religious sites with no problem, not only in secular Syria, but also in theocratic Iran—churches, synagogues and mosques. Most Muslims feel more respect towards Judaism and Christianity than we do. Despite their rejection of American foreign policy, they admire the West in many respects. Young Muslims like to wear (fake) Western sneakers, jeans and T-shirts. While retaining their faith, they would like to be like us in many ways—free, modern and, on their terms, democratic. They would like to like America, once the great beacon of hope for oppressed people around the world, were it not for its blood-drenched foreign policy.

The Muslim world is nothing like the way it is depicted in the Western media. Western television broadcasters show a manufactured, distorted image of mobs raging against the West. In September 2001, after the attacks on the World Trade Center, many television stations showed Palestinian children rejoicing. But the footage had been staged. According to reports in the Israeli newspaper *Haaretz*, the children had been given sweets so that they would rejoice in front of the cameras.[64]

"Spontaneous" anti-Western demonstrations in the Muslim world usually take place only when they are carefully organized and staged in cooperation with Western broadcasters. As soon as the cameras are turned off, the "TV demonstrators" are given a little baksheesh and are taken back home in the same trucks that brought them.

In contrast to the West, xenophobia is unknown in the Muslim world. We may be economically and technologically more advanced than these countries—but not in human terms. When it comes to kindness and love of one's neighbor, a sense of family, and hospitality, we could learn a lot from Muslims.

This cordiality can, as in the case of Iraq, turn into raging anger when the West yet again scornfully tramples upon the rights of Muslims. Jean-Paul Sartre described this self-destructive despair during the Algerian war of liberation in 1961: "The repressed rage, never managing to explode, goes round in circles and wreaks havoc on the oppressed themselves. In order to rid themselves of it, they end up massacring each other, tribes battle one against the other since they cannot confront the real enemy—and you can count on colonial policy to fuel rivalries; ... the torrent of violence to sweep away all barriers. ... It is the age of the boomerang; the third stage of violence: it flies right back at us, it strikes us and, once again, we have no idea what hits us."[65]

Does that not sound rather like a description of the situation in Iraq in after the American invasion? The "coalition of the willing" has taken from the Iraqis everything that might have given them the opportunity to be as "noble, helpful and good" as we like to perceive ourselves. It has destroyed all their state structures; it has trampled upon their dignity and pride. It has systematically incited Iraqis to turn on each other.

It is so hypocritical of the West to then be "amazed" that the strategy really works and that the despair of Iraqis sometimes even turns into self-destruction. It is absurd to claim that "something like that could never happen here"—a claim often uttered with an undertone of racist disgust.

Just consider how a power outage in New York in 1977 and a hurricane in New Orleans in 2005 were enough to trigger widespread looting, murder and mayhem. *Homo homini lupus*—"Man to Man is an arrant Wolfe" (Thomas Hobbes). This is true, not only of Muslims, but of Jews and Christians as well.

III.

Terrorists in Islamic disguise are murderers. The same holds true for the ringleaders disguised as Christians who wage illegal wars.

The attacks carried out since the mid-1990s by Arab terrorists on Western facilities are in their view a response to the never-ending "organized robbery and murder" on the part of the West. The attacks, including those on the World Trade Center, have killed more than 5,000 Western civilians. They are morally completely unacceptable. The end never justifies the means.

That is why the attacks on the World Trade Center were condemned by almost all Muslim governments, by Syria and Iran,[66] even by Hizbollah[67] and Hamas.[68] In many Muslim countries distraught people laid flowers in front of the U.S. embassy.[69] Terrorists who kill innocent people are not freedom fighters or resistance fighters, holy warriors or martyrs. They are murderers.

But are not those who mastermind illegal wars of aggression[70] also terrorists and murderers, who even murder their own soldiers? If one talks about the 5,000 Westerners murdered by Al-Qaeda, must one not also talk about the hundreds of thousands of Iraqi civilians who have been killed in George W. Bush's illegal war?

Do not the legal yardsticks we apply to Saddam Hussein, Slobodan Milosevic or Omar al-Bashir also apply to Western heads of governments? Why do Western elites not even dare to *ask* whether George W. Bush and Tony Blair should be brought before an international criminal court because of the war in Iraq that is based on lies?[71] Does international law not apply to Westerners? Why are victors never tried for their war crimes?

In the opinion of the Nuremberg war crimes tribunal, "To initiate a war of aggression, therefore, is not only an international crime: it is the supreme international crime differing only from other war crimes in that it contains within it the accumulated evil of all crimes of war."[72] The chief U.S. prosecutor Robert H. Jackson[73] stated: "We must never forget that the record on which we judge these defendants is the record on which history will judge us tomorrow."[74]

"Wars of aggression are the terrorism of the rich," as Peter Ustinov put it.[75] For an Iraqi child, it makes no difference whether he is blown apart by an "Islamic" suicide bomber or a "Christian" bomb. For this child, George W. Bush and Tony Blair are just as much terrorists as Bin Laden is for us.

The high number of civilian victims of military operations is often excused with the argument that such "collateral damage" is not premeditated. That is disingenuous—at least with respect to aerial attacks—because the death of civilians is almost always tacitly accepted in such cases. Tacit acceptance (*dolus eventualis*) is regarded in advanced legal systems as acting with intent.[76]

Aerial bombardment is, moreover, rarely effective. Special-forces operations on the ground can usually achieve much more. But then one would have to accept a greater number of fatalities within one's own ranks. And that could cost votes. So instead one drops cluster bombs and tacitly accepts the death of civilians. Dropping cluster bombs from the safety of a pilot's cockpit is the most cowardly form of terrorism on the part of the powerful.

The myth of the honorable war is mankind's greatest lie. "*Dulce bellum inexpertis*—War is only sweet to those who have not experienced it" (Erasmus of Rotterdam).

Armed resistance to wars and occupation that are illegal under international law is nonetheless only legitimate if it is conducted in accordance with the humanitarian law that applies in armed conflicts. Suicide attacks on civilians, who have different beliefs, such as we see every day in Iraq and elsewhere, are acts of terrorism. They have nothing to do with legitimate resistance.

The most spectacular attacks on civilians in Iraq are, however, for the most part directed from outside the country. According to a statement issued on July 11, 2007, by the spokesman for the multi-national forces in Iraq, General Kevin Bergner, between 80 and 90 percent of the suicide bombers come from abroad.[77]

One must clearly distinguish between this almost entirely foreign terrorism directed against civilians and the legitimate multi-confessional Iraqi resistance to foreign occupation. Nobody can take away from the Iraqis their right to resist. It is a timeless inviolable right of all peoples, guaranteed by Article 51 of the UN Charter.

The great majority of the Iraqi people support the resistance movement, which explicitly rejects attacks on civilians. The resistance not only involves Sunni and Shi'ite Muslims, but Christians as well.[78] The number of Christian resistance fighters in Iraq is greater than the number of Al-Qaeda fighters. Women also fight in the multi-confessional Iraqi resistance.[79]

Is that really surprising? What would we do if there were enemy tanks on our streets? Are only those resistance fighters who are on our side "freedom fighters" and the rest "terrorists"?

The Iraqis have long since lost the media war. There are still at least 50 military operations conducted by occupation forces against the Iraqi civilian population every day, and an even higher number of counter-attacks every day by the resistance on occupation forces and their allies.[80] The daily count of suicide attacks against civilians is one, two or three at most.

Nevertheless, TV broadcasters show almost exclusively pictures of such suicide terror attacks, which are carried out mainly by foreigners, as if they were typical of the Iraqis' struggle against the United States.[81] They therefore convey a completely distorted picture of the situation in Iraq.[82] We do not get to see the true face of this war. The Pentagon has a monopoly on information in occupied Iraq, and exploits this to the full.

Of course, non-violent resistance in the spirit of Mahatma Gandhi or Martin Luther King would be preferable to violent resistance, even when it is legitimate. In the religious war between the city states of Mecca and Medina, Muhammad's most fascinating victory came when, to the amazement of his enemies in Mecca, he and his followers gathered, unarmed, outside the gates of Mecca and demanded access to the holy sites.[83]

Passive resistance born of the power of faith would also make the Iraqi resistance more credible. But for centuries have we not shown the world that only brute force guarantees success?

IV.

Muslims were and are at least as tolerant as Jews and Christians. They have made major contributions to Western civilization.

It was not Muslims who invented "holy war," joined Crusades under the rallying cry "*Deus lo vult*—God wills it" (Urban II)[84] and in the process massacred more than four million Muslims and Jews.[85] It was not Muslims who waded "ankle-deep in blood" in Jerusalem before they "rejoicing and weeping from excess of happiness … came to worship and give thanks at the sepulcher of our savior Jesus," as a contemporary reported.[86]

Islam never associates the word "holy" with war. Jihad means "exertion, a struggle on the pathways of God" (Hans Küng),[87] an effort that can involve defensive war. Nowhere in the Qur'an does jihad mean "holy war." Wars are never "holy," only a just peace is holy.[88]

Nor was it Muslims who massacred up to 50 million people in the name of colonizing Africa and Asia.[89] It was not Muslims who instigated the First and Second World Wars, in which almost 70 million people perished. And it was not Muslims, but Germans, who ignominiously murdered six million Jews—fellow citizens, friends and neighbors—in an industrially organized breach of civilization.[90] No other culture has been more violent and bloody over the past centuries as Western civilization. When have so-called "Christian" politicians ever honored Christianity, this wonderful religion of love?

Nobody can deny that the territorial expansion of the Muslim dynasties between the 7th and 17th centuries—like that of the European powers over the same period—was conducted also with the sword. On the Muslim side, there were inexcusable massacres.

Muslim conquerors did not however, as a rule, attempt to force Christians or Jews to accept Islam, expel them, or exterminate them. When Saladin won back Jerusalem after a hard-fought battle in 1187, he made a point of not exacting revenge and let the Christians go free in exchange for a ransom. He even waived the ransom for poor Christians.

Tolerance towards Christians and Jews was the law and the pride of Muslim civilization.[91] Under Muslim rule entire peoples remained Christian or Jewish, while the "Christian" Inquisition burned those who held different beliefs at the stake.

When the Muslim general Tariq ibn Ziyad landed on the Iberian Peninsula in 711, a period of cultural and scientific blossom began, which was to last for more than seven centuries and contribute enormously to Western civilization. In Andalusia, then the most modern state in Europe, the coexistence of Muslims, Jews and Christians proved to be an unparalleled success. Jews fared much better under Muslim rule than under "Christian" hegemony.

It was only when the "Christian" King Ferdinand of Aragon

completed the Reconquista in 1492 by taking Granada, the last Muslim bastion in Spain, that the merciless expulsion of Jews began. Hundreds of thousands of Jews were forced to leave the country. For centuries Jews had been respected, held high office, and lived together in harmony with their Muslim contemporaries. Most fled to Muslim countries around the Mediterranean.

The coexistence of Christians, Jews and Muslims in Muslim countries only became troubled with the advent of colonialism and nationalism in the 19th and 20th centuries, when some Muslims came to see Christians and Jews as party to aggressive Western imperialism. The Armenian tragedy in Turkey was a result of nationalist, not religious intolerance.[92]

Muslims in the enlightened Andalusian era not only salvaged for us the sunken treasures of Greek and Roman culture and philosophy, they also created new sciences. They pioneered experimental optics, invented the compass, discovered the paths of the planets and crucial elements of modern medicine and pharmacy. Even if we do not want to believe it: We live in a culture that was formed by Judaism, Christianity AND Islam.[93]

V.

Love of God and love of one's neighbor are the central commandments not only in the Bible but also in the Qur'an.

A comparison of the texts shows that the Qur'an is at least as tolerant as the Old and New Testaments. God and his prophets do sometimes express themselves in very martial tones in all three scriptures. In the Old Testament Book of Numbers 31:7, 15, 17 it is written: "They did battle against Midian, as the Lord had commanded Moses, and killed every male. ... Moses said to them, 'Have you allowed all the women to live? ... Now therefore, kill every male among the little ones, and kill every woman who has known a man by sleeping with him.'" [94]

In the New Testament, Jesus is quoted in Matthew 10:34 as having said: "Do not think that I have come to bring peace to the earth; I have not come to bring peace, but a sword." [95] In his *Table Talk* the powerfully eloquent Protestant Martin Luther said: "One may give short shrift to heretics. While they perish at the stake, the faithful should destroy the evil by the root and bathe their hands in the blood of the bishops and the pope." [96]

Surah 4:89 of the Qur'an is no less violent: "They but wish that ye should reject Faith, as they do. ... Take ... not friends from their ranks until they flee in the way of God (from what is forbidden). But if they turn renegades, seize them and slay them wherever ye find them." [97]

Extremists and preachers of hate in East and West almost always ignore the historical context of these passages. Moses, Jesus and Muhammad were not born in a historical vacuum but into a belligerent world. At first glance, the Old Testament, especially in its historical passages, might seem to be the bloodiest of the three holy books—much bloodier than the Qur'an.

But anybody who has studied the Old Testament knows that its central commandment—apart from the commandment to love God and justice—is: "You shall love your neighbor as yourself" (Leviticus 19:18). [98] For Christians too, love of one's neighbor and justice are the most important commandments after the love of God (Matthew 5:6, 5:10).[99]

The Qur'an tells Muslims to "Do good … to neighbors who are near, or neighbors who are strangers" (Surah 4:36).[100] Islam also endorses the "Ten Commandments," including the prohibition on killing[101]—with the sole exception of the commandment to observe the Sabbath, as according to the Islamic view God did not need a day of rest after creating the world.[102] The Qur'an calls for "more humanity and more justice" (Hans Küng).[103]

The main problem with the Western debate about the Qur'an is that everybody talks about it but hardly anybody has read it. The bellicose passages in the Qur'an have to do with "the religious wars of the period between Mecca and Medina and therefore only (have to do with) the people of Mecca and Medina of the period," as the Egyptian minister of religious affairs Mahmoud Zakzouk has correctly pointed out.[104]

In Surah 29:46 it is written: "Our God and your God is one,"[105] even though God is called Jehovah in Hebrew and Allah in Arabic—by Arab Christians as well.[106] We are all children of Abraham. Is it not outrageous blasphemy when Jews, Christians or Muslims misuse the Bible and the Qur'an as a weapon, in order to hammer home their particular view of this one God?

Terrorism is never religious. To be a terrorist is to adopt the methods of the devil; no terrorist may invoke God. There is no "Islamic" terrorism, just as the terrorism of the IRA in Northern Ireland was never "Christian" or "Catholic," There is merely terrorism that bears an Islamic mask, and it does not lead to paradise, but to hell, as do wars of aggression that bear a Christian or democratic mask.

The claim that violence is above all a religious problem is an atheist myth. People committed murder before religion existed and have continued to do so ever since. The mass murder of the Nazis and of the Soviet and Chinese Communists are the sad proof that man is the cruelest creature—with and without religion.[107]

The shocking fascination of contemporary suicide terrorism is based on two kinds of shamelessness: the shamelessness of some Western politicians who continue to spill Muslim blood at a ratio of 10:1, and the shamelessness with which those who mastermind terrorism distort the Qur'an and try to make young Muslims believe that all they have to do to become Islamic martyrs is blow themselves up as suicide bombers.

VI.

Western policies towards the Muslim world suffer from a shocking ignorance of even the simplest facts.

Almost nobody in the West knows that there are 30 churches in Teheran and that Christian children receive instruction in their own religion. There are also 15 synagogues in the Iranian capital and about 4,000 Jewish children go to Jewish schools. There are kosher butchers, kosher restaurants and a Jewish hospital, to which even notorious troublemaker Mahmoud Ahmadinejad donated some money.[108]

The 25,000 Jews have a constitutional right to a representative in parliament, similar to the Christians.[109] In 1979, shortly after the revolution, Ayatollah Khomeini even issued a fatwa decreeing that Jews were to be protected. His words are painted on the walls of many Iranian synagogues: "We respect religious minorities. They are part of our people. Islam does not sanction their oppression."[110]

Relations between Jews and Persians have been good since ancient times. It was the Persian king Cyrus the Great[111] who in 538 BC freed the Jews from their Babylonian captivity. The Bible calls him a "shepherd loved and anointed by God."[112]

It is true that as protected minorities, Jews and Christians in Iran do not enjoy the same political rights (and duties) as do Muslims. But do we really grant Muslims the same rights as Christians and Jews in their everyday lives in Europe? Does Israel really grant its fellow Arab citizens the same rights in daily life as its Jewish citizens?

Ahmadinejad has indeed made vicious "anti-Zionist," anti-Israeli statements,[113] which on top of that were falsely translated in the West. However, his aggressive stance, which is rich in political folly and poor in historical understanding, finds little support among the Iranian people and has even earned him the rebuke of Iran's spiritual leadership.[114]

This anti-Zionism, however, is not to be equated with hatred of Jews or anti-Semitism. Orthodox Jews, such as the Hasidic Satmar community, also reject an Israeli state "before the advent of the Messiah" and thus also represent an "anti-Zionist" position.[115]

In Iran and other Muslim states there has never been real anti-Semitism or persecution of Jews by the state, as was the case in Europe. During the Nazi era many European Jews fled to freedom via Iran. Jews in Iran are respected citizens. As Ciamak

Morsathegh, the Jewish director of the Jewish hospital in Tehran, put it: "Anti-Semitism is not an Islamic, but a European phenomenon."[116]

That is no excuse for Ahmadinejad's provocations. By making lots of noise on the foreign-policy front, he is seeking to divert attention from his policy failures at home. In February 2007, the conservative Iranian newspaper *Jomhuri-ye Eslami* rightly complained of his "repulsive tone" that "unnecessarily gives the international community an impression of hostility" and called on him to stay away from "rabble-rousing and sloganeering."[117]

And *those* of the mullahs, who are responsible for Iran's repressive system, are also extremely unpopular among Iran's young people. They see these *repressive* mullahs as relicts of the past and they consider their repressiveness an annoying hindrance to progress. The revolutionary religious fervor of the late '70s and early '80s has long since been extinguished.[118]

For eight years before Ahmadinejad came to power, Iran had a cosmopolitan reformist head of government, Mohammad Khatami. He stood for democracy, human rights, and the enhancement of women's rights. But much to the annoyance of the U.S. government he was independent-minded and not its puppet.[119] The United States never gave him a chance. Khatami's lack of success in foreign policy and at home was one of the main reasons why so many pro-reform middle-class Iranians did not vote in 2005—which led to Ahmadinejad's surprise election victory.

The West itself contributed to the rise of this rowdy demagogue. Nonetheless, Iran, with its great and ancient civilization and its charming and distinguished people, deserves a more cosmopolitan and tolerant government that respects human rights. But is that not true of many a Western country as well? And isn't that why America elected Barack Obama as its new president?

Western ignorance of the Muslim world is also evident in much more banal issues than the Iran conflict—for example, in the view, widely held in Europe, that the Muslim headscarf is a "symbol of the oppression of women."[120] On this issue the United States is much more tolerant. The U.S. Department of Justice has stated that the intolerance evident in banning headscarves "is un-American, and is morally despicable."[121]

The German weekly *Die Zeit* jokingly commented on the crusade to free Europe of the headscarf: "If you ask five Muslim women why they wear a headscarf, you will get five different answers: One covers her head for God; another because the scarf goes well with her fashionable H&M clothes; the third will reveal herself to be an ardent feminist; the fourth cites traditions in her village; while the fifth is defying her ultra-secular mother, who has forbidden her to wear a headscarf."[122]

Of course, forcing anyone to wear a headscarf is unacceptable. But is not forcing anyone to take it off just as unacceptable?

The debates about forced marriage, female circumcision, or honor killing are also conducted with a shocking degree of ignorance. There is nothing in the Qur'an or the Hadeeth[123] of Muhammad about these completely unacceptable misogynist practices. They derive from a pre-Islamic patriarchal and heathen era.

Some of these practices are several thousand years old—the gruesome "pharaonic" circumcision of women, for example. This brutal mutilation is not only practiced in Muslim countries such as

Egypt and Sudan, but also in predominantly Christian countries such as Ethiopia and Kenya. The victims are Muslims, Christians, Jewish Falashas, as well as members of other religions.

So-called honor killings unfortunately also occur among Christians—for example, in such Christian countries as Brazil, Argentina and Venezuela.[124] Most Muslim (and Christian) governments rightly take legal measures to counter these deplorable pre-Islamic and un-Islamic customs and crimes.

In some Muslim countries the advancement of women has gone much further in certain respects than in the West. In Egypt, 30 percent of all professors are women; in Germany the figure is only 15 percent.[125] In Iran well over 60 percent of students are women, which has prompted the introduction of a 30 percent quota for men.[126] There is also a longer tradition of female heads of government in Muslim countries than in the West.

Nonetheless, a lot still needs to be done if women are to attain full and equal rights in all Muslim countries, particularly in our partner countries Saudi Arabia and Afghanistan, but also in Iran. However, that is not a problem with Islam. It is a political problem and one that has to do with antiquated patriarchal social structures.

The fact that in the Western countries, public and private shelters for battered women are bursting at the seams shows that even in the presumed modern societies of the West violence against women is a grievous social problem that has not yet been resolved.

We should mind our own business and examine ourselves more closely: Until 1957 a German man had the legal "right of directive" to decide whether his wife may go to work.[127] Until 1970 the men of Switzerland refused to give women the right to vote—after all, both the Old and the New Testament demand the submission of woman to the will of man (see Genesis 3:16 and 1 Corinthians 14:34 f.).[128]

Whoever wants to see an end to hatred and intolerance should above all overcome their own ignorance. Everybody has the right to his or her own opinions, but definitely not to his or her own facts. What is to prevent us from traveling to Syria or Iran to form our own opinions on that alien and purportedly so dangerous world? The streets of Damascus and Tehran are much safer than the streets of New York or Detroit.

According to United Nations statistics, in 2006 the homicide rate in the United States was 5.9 per 100,000 inhabitants. In Iran the rate was 2.93 and in Syria 1.4. Most Muslim countries are safer than the United States, even safer than Switzerland, where the rate is 2.94 per 100,000 inhabitants.[129]

Why don't we start intercultural dialog in our own personal environment? Why not expand student exchange programs between Muslim and Christian countries—or even with Israel? Why not get to know some works of wonderful Arabic literature or read the famous Ring Parable in *Nathan the Wise* by the great German writer of the Enlightenment era, Gotthold Ephraim Lessing? [130] There, a father (God) bequeathes to each of the three sons he loves equally (Judaism, Christianity and Islam) an identical ring. One ring is the original; it has the ability to render its owner pleasant in the eyes of God and mankind. The other two are replicas.

The brothers call on a judge to establish which of them has the original. The judge, with the wisdom of Solomon, explains that the bearer of the authentic ring is he who earns the love of his fellow men.

For German chancellor Angela Merkel, the most beautiful passage in the play is when the Muslim Saladin calls out to the Jew Nathan "be my friend!" [131] Could we not all learn from this ancient Sephardic Jewish parable and its dream of a peaceful competition among these religions?

VII.

The West must treat the Muslim world just as fairly and as generously as it treats Israel. Muslims are worth as much as Jews and Christians.

With a mixture of self-righteousness, ignorance and hatred, many people in the West think Islam is a bloodthirsty religion and that Muslims are potential terrorists who are hostile towards democracy, women, Jews and Christians.

The friend and spiritual advisor of the former President George W. Bush, Frank Graham, has called Islam "a very evil and wicked religion." [132] Bill O'Reilly, TV idol of American conservatives, has said: "We cannot intervene in the Muslim world ever again. What we can do is bomb the living daylights out of them." [133]

American television commentator Ann Coulter thinks: "We should invade their countries, kill their leaders and convert them to Christianity." She also says: "Perhaps we could put aside our national, ongoing post-9/11 Muslim butt-kissing contest and get on with the business at hand: Bombing Syria back to the Stone

Age and then permanently disarming Iran."[134] The list of such statements could be extended indefinitely.

Just imagine for a moment that Graham, O'Reilly or Coulter had said "Judaism" instead of "Islam" and "Israel" instead of "Muslim countries." There would have been a storm of protest, and quite rightly so. Why may one say fascistic things about Muslims and their religion, while any such comments about Christians or Jews would be rejected as entirely unacceptable, and rightly so?[135]

We must end this demonization of Islam and Muslims. It is not only shameful, it also harms our interests.

The deepening divide between Orient and Occident also endangers the security of Israel. The strongest long-term guarantee for the survival of Israel and its five million Jews is not the enmity, but the friendship of its 300 million immediate and more distant Arab neighbors.[136] To attain this, the West, but also Israel, must make a fair contribution.

The Jewish people did not attain its moral stature because of its military victories or because of the impressive number of its talents. It attained its moral uniqueness through its piety, wisdom, humanism and creativity, as well as through its long, brave and often cunning struggle for justice and against oppression.

It is understandable that after the Holocaust Israel has sought to ensure its military strength—and to defend its legitimate interests with great vigor, even severity. But severity without justice is a strategy that is doomed to failure. If all the creative country of Israel does is destroy, it will destroy itself as well.

Israel—and the entire Western world—must invest at least as much in justice as in weapons. The treatment of the Palestinians is not compatible with the moral stature and uniqueness of the Jewish people. This is the only conclusion one may come to, especially as an admirer of Jewish culture.

The Palestinians must also change their policies. The West is right to demand that they renounce violence against Israel. But should it not also demand that Israel renounces violence against the Palestinians? According to the Israeli human-rights organization B'Tselem, in 2007 13 Israelis were killed in the Israeli-Palestinian conflict, while 384 Palestinians were killed by Israeli security forces.[137]

Reconciliation between Jews and Arabs is just as possible as the miraculous reconciliation between the Germans and the French proved to be. Jews and Arabs have more in common in religious, cultural and historical terms than most people realize. As Israeli President Shimon Peres put it, they "have the same parents, Abraham and Moses."[138]

For centuries both Jews and Arabs were persecuted—and not only during the Crusades and the Reconquista. The Vichy government in France, for example, applied the same racist discriminatory laws to Jews that had been "successfully" tested on Algerians (Olivier Le Cour Grandmaison).[139]

Germans, myself included, have an historical responsibility towards Israel and its right to exist—in the past, the present and the future. Because of its history and everything it has gone through over the millennia, the Jewish people deserve a secure home in Palestine.

But for the very same reason we also have an historical responsibility towards the Palestinians. They are paying the price for the guilt

Germany will always bear because of the Holocaust. The Jewish political scientist Alfred Grosser is surely right when he said: "Whoever wants to shake off Hitler, must (also) defend the Palestinians."[140]

The true lesson of the Holocaust is that we may never just stand by and watch passively as people are oppressed, stripped of their rights and humiliated. We should have stood up for the Jewish people back then when they were weak, and not only nowadays, when they are strong and influential. Belated courage is the opportunist brother of cowardice.

It is a bizarre spectacle to observe certain Western politicians fight ever more resolutely and courageously year after year against past injustice, while remaining inexcusably silent about present injustice.[141] One can also be guilty of not saying a word.

The challenge of our era is to help heal the wounds in the Middle East—by means of security guarantees for Israel, to which Europe must provide a robust military contribution, but also through helping to establish a viable Palestinian state. We must build bridges, not walls.

A model Palestinian state, that is backed by the West and acknowledges Israel's right to exist within just borders, and that opposes all forms of terrorism really would mark a new start for the Middle East—and for the relationship between the Western world and the Muslim world. We cannot continue on our current path.

The "wars on terror" against the Muslim countries Afghanistan and Iraq have already cost $1.6 trillion, which is more than the Vietnam War cost.[142] The United States spends more than $100 billion on the war in Iraq each year, but less than $5 billion for economic reconstruction there.[143]

In light of these figures, can one seriously ask what a successful alternative to the current "anti-terror" policies might look like? We have to turn the ratio around. We have to treat the Muslim world just as fairly and as generously as we—quite rightly—treat Israel. We must ultimately deprive international terrorism of any arguments in its defense.

VIII.

Muslims must champion a progressive and tolerant Islam, as did their Prophet Muhammad. They must strip terrorism of its religious mask.

Not only the West, but also the Muslim world needs to change its behavior in a fundamental way. While retaining their religious identity, Muslims must show more courage in standing up for freedom and the rule of law; for a political and economic system that fosters individual talent rather than stifling it; for the full and equal rights of men and women; for real freedom of religion also for Jews and Christians—for a tolerant progressive and modern understanding of the teachings of Islam. The many millions of Muslims living in the West could play an important part in this process.

Muslims must interpret the fascinating message of their Prophet Muhammad for the modern world and continue with the social reforms he risked his life for. They must throw overboard the pre-Islamic ballast that is impeding a renaissance of Islamic civilization. They must create an educated elite that can lead the Muslim world successfully into the third millennium.

Muhammad, market economy, and modernity can fit together very well.

Unlike many Muslim politicians of our day, Muhammad was not a reactionary.[144] Unlike them, he did not long to be transported back 1,400 years. He was a bold, forward-looking egalitarian revolutionary, who had the courage to break the bounds of tradition. His Islam was not a religion of stasis or regression, but of renewal and new departures. Even a little of this great reformer's dynamism would do the Muslim world a lot of good—a world that at least in part is submerged in fatalism and self-pity.

Muhammad fought passionately for social change. He stood up for the poor and the weak and—to the annoyance of many of his male followers—for a massive improvement in the rights of women, who in pre-Islamic times in almost all cultures enjoyed virtually no rights at all. Men who oppress women may not claim to have the backing of Muhammad or the Qur'an.

Muhammad was—like our Jewish forefathers Abraham, Moses and King Solomon, who according to the Bible had a thousand wives and concubines—married to several women,[145] one of whom was Jewish and another Christian. Muhammad warned his followers: "Whoever wrongs a Jew or a Christian, will have to face me on the Day of Judgment."[146] It would be good if some Muslim extremists took the prophet's wise words to heart.

Muhammad was neither a fanatic nor an extremist. He wanted to tell the polytheist Arabs of his day about the God of the Jews and the Christians—in authentic, pure form. The Qur'an is in part a wonderful retelling of the central messages of the Bible: "And before this was the Book of Moses as a guide and a mercy:

And this Book confirms (it) in the Arabic tongue" (Surah 46:12).
For Muslims, the Qur'an is the "Newest Testament."

Muhammad repeatedly proclaimed that Jesus would rise
again before the Last Judgment: "How happy you will be when
the son of Mary descends to you."[147] Jesus and Mary are described
in the Qur'an with great love as "signs for all peoples" (Surah
21:91).[148] The Qur'an also treats the great Jewish prophets, especially Moses, as role models. "A Muslim who does not believe
in Muhammad's precursors Moses and Jesus is not a Muslim"
(Mahmoud Zakzouk).[149]

Today's terrorism is an absurd distortion of Muhammad's
teachings. It is a crime against Islam. Islam means submission to
God and peace. The Muslim world may not permit its great and
proud religion, with its ethos of humanity and justice, to be sullied
by raging terrorists whose hearts and minds are filled with hatred.

Nobody has caused greater damage to the standing of Islam
in the course of its history, which spans almost fourteen centuries, than terrorists pretending to be Muslims. The Muslim world
must strip the religious mask from the face of the terrorists.

IX.

**Nothing fosters terrorism more than the West's "war on
terror." Wars of aggression are not only the most immoral,
but also the least intelligent way to combat terrorism.**

The West's claim that Muslims have to finally clarify their relationship towards violence, applies equally to the West itself. We

must unmask the West's warriors of aggression. We must show the infinite stupidity of their strategy. Terrorism in the guise of Islam is an ideology; ideologies cannot be shot down. One has to undermine its foundations, to prove it wrong.

In early 2001, radical Islamism around the world was on the ropes. The dream of solving Iran's or Afghanistan's political problems by means of a process of radical Islamization had turned into a nightmare. Muslims had come to the bitter realization that the hardline Mullahs had turned some of their countries into grim (religious) police states.[150] During the United States's blitzkrieg, the Afghan people demonstratively left the Taliban to their fate—an unusual event in the history of Afghanistan.[151]

In light of this evident failure of radical Islamism, Al-Qaeda's attack on New York and Washington was not just an act of revenge but also an attempt to regain the high ground. Through an act of such diabolical boldness and the ensuing media spectacle, the radical Islamists wanted to win back the sympathy of the masses. They wanted to provoke the United States into overreacting, which would in turn give radical Islamism a new impetus.

The whole scenario is made all the more absurd by the fact that the hawks of the U.S. government had been keenly awaiting just such an opportunity. Al-Qaeda wanted to provoke, and the Bush administration was just waiting to be provoked.

Al-Qaeda's strategy worked perfectly. The countless bombs that rained down on the heads of Afghan civilians, who were already tired of the Taliban, revived prostrate radical Islamism and helped it back on its feet. The Afghans certainly wanted to get rid of the Taliban and Al-Qaeda—both groups that had been created by the intelligence agencies of the United States, Saudi Arabia and Pakistan—but they did not see why thousands of Afghan civilians had to be bombed to death to achieve that goal.[152]

None of the terrorists who attacked the World Trade Center were from Afghanistan or Iraq. They came from Saudi Arabia, Germany, the United Emirates, Lebanon and Egypt.[153] In order to neutralize their Saudi Arabian ideological leader Osama Bin Laden at his retreat in the mountains of the Hindu Kush, more intelligent methods could have been adopted than bombing Kabul.

So the radical Islamists once again had reason to issue a worldwide call-to-arms against the foreign invaders and against their own authoritarian pro-Western governments—just as they had done in 1979 when the Soviets marched in.

The election victories of Hamas, the rise of radical Islamism in the once secular Iraq, and the resurgence of the Taliban in Afghanistan have a lot to do with the brutality and stupidity of the wars on terror.

Radical forces in the West and in the Muslim world have spurred each other on. Bin Laden and Ahmadinejad provided George W. Bush with his best catch phrases, and vice versa. We must break through this fatal reciprocity as swiftly as possible.

The West does not have the right to take military action all over the world against radical Islamist movements—or against leftwing radical or rightwing radical organizations. It does not have the right to turn the world into a bloody and chaotic battlefield in order to impose its vision of the world. Western combat troops have no business fighting in Iraq, Afghanistan or Iran.

The Muslim countries must solve their problems with radical

Islamism primarily by themselves. Even where radical Islamism degenerates into terrorism, it is first and foremost the task of national forces to combat it. Only in extreme and exceptional cases and with the backing of the United Nations Security Council should international police task forces provide reinforcement.

The damage foreign military interventions cause is almost always greater than the benefit, even when the motives are honest and humanitarian. It is not enough to *want* to do good; one has to actually *do* good.

The war on terrorism will not be won by military means—neither in the Hindu Kush nor in Baghdad. It will be won in the hearts and minds of the world's 1.4 billion Muslims, who live in the East and the West, the North and the South, and who are observing the politics of the West very closely.

Terrorism grows with every Muslim child killed by a Western bomb. With each day that passes, we are sinking deeper into the morass of our own policies.

It is above all aerial warfare that has failed miserably as a means of fighting terrorism. Despite continuous aerial bombardment Bin Laden managed to escape from Tora Bora, because there were more journalists than American soldiers surrounding the cave complex where he was believed to be hiding.[154] At about the same time, the Taliban leader Mullah Omar succeeded in breaking through the thin ranks of the U.S. forces on a motorbike.[155]

Tora Bora is a grotesque symbol of the folly of the anti-terror crusade. Not even Cervantes, the creator of Don Quixote, could have dreamed up a more bizarre slapstick finale.

X.

What is needed now is the art of statesmanship, not the art of war—in the Iran conflict, in the Iraq conflict, in the Afghanistan conflict, and in the Palestine conflict.

The almost childish refusal of the former American president to talk directly to politicians he did not like such as Arafat, Assad, Saddam or Ahmadinejad, along with the decision—taken after consultations with God—to develop strategies to bomb them out of office, were two of the most absurd and wrong-headed decisions of our time.[156]

"A statesman who seeks to promote peace must talk to the statesman in the opposing camp" (Helmut Schmidt, former German chancellor).[157] It was only possible to resolve the East-West conflict of the post-war years because Ronald Reagan never felt squeamish about meeting with the rulers of what he termed the "evil empire."[158]

It is simply not true that, for example, in the Iran conflict there is, apart from the strategy of imposing ever-tougher sanctions, only the "catastrophic alternative" of an "Iranian bomb or bombing Iran" (Nicolas Sarkozy).[159] The real alternative to the ostracism and demonization of a great nation such as Iran is its reintegration into the community of nations—with all the same rights and the same obligations as any other member.

The main reason Iran is a problem for the West is that by marginalizing it and severing ties—in order to punish it for deposing the pro-Western Shah and his regime—the West has forfeited any influence it might have had on the political decision-making processes within Iran. This development is not irreversible. There is a wise saying: "If you cannot beat your enemy, embrace him."

The majority of Iranians are pro-Western. They are waiting for the West and they pin their hopes on the West. But they do not pin their hopes on the West's bombs, which would yet again primarily kill the innocent, or on an invasion by Western soldiers, but on an "invasion" of Western businesspeople and tourists.

Even Shirin Ebadi, a prominent critic of the Iranian regime and a Nobel Peace Prize laureate, argues passionately against any such military action by the U.S., because it would "thwart virtually all the efforts that Iranians have undertaken to promote democracy in recent years."[160]

The complex problems facing the Middle East can only be solved by political means. The best way to tackle them would be with a long-term conference for the whole region modeled on the Commission on Security and Cooperation in Europe (CSCE).[161] Besides the UN Security Council, all the major players in the region should be represented—including Syria and Iran, Israel and the democratically elected representatives of Palestine, and the leadership of the legitimate Iraqi resistance.

A solution to the Iraq conflict will only be found if the United States negotiates—as it did in the Vietnam War—with the leaders of the resistance, though of course not with Al-Qaeda. The leaders of the patriotic and moderate Islamist resistance are almost all prepared to take part in such talks.

Just as in the East-West conflict of the 1970s and 1980s, tough but fair negotiations now present a real alternative to irresponsible wars and equally irresponsible passivity. All parties would benefit from such an approach, as has proven to be the case with the CSCE process. After one and a half decades of difficult negotiations it brought freedom, human rights, democracy and increasing prosperity to Eastern Europe. The CSCE process brought to Europe as a whole stability, freedom and disarmament. "Mortal enemies became friends—without a single shot being fired" (former German foreign minister Hans-Dietrich Genscher).[162]

That should be the goal of a "Middle East CSCE." Perhaps one day a common economic area, or even more, will emerge in the region. Who would have thought 60 years ago that there could ever be a united Europe? Politics requires vision, and that holds true for the Middle East as well.

In view of the massive military superiority of the United States, how one can compare such a policy of negotiations to the scary "policy of appeasement" before the Second World War remains a secret of the neocons. It would not be "appeasement" if the current U.S. leadership stopped inventing more and more horror stories about Muslim countries, or if it stopped bombing a path to the natural resources of the world—if it stopped destroying the great values for which so many people once loved America and would love to love America again.[163]

Which Muslim country could hope to attack either the West or Israel with even a remote prospect of success, given the overwhelming nuclear and also conventional second-strike capability of the United States and of Israel?

Even if Iran had nuclear weapons—and that would certainly

not be a desirable state of affairs—the basics of nuclear strategy would still apply: Whoever shoots first, dies second. Whoever attacks the United States or Israel with a nuclear bomb, might as well blow themselves up straightaway.

In terms of numbers, the United States has the nuclear weaponry to kill 20 billion people.[164] That means it could burn to a cinder all 70 million Iranians three hundred times over. Iran knows that—even its loud president knows that. His defense budget is just one hundredth of that of the United States.[165]

Unlike the major Western powers, Iran has not attacked any other country during the past 150 years,[166] though it has been attacked several times—also with the help of the West. There are still 400,000 Iranians who were severely wounded or injured in the war with Iraq, among them 50,000 victims of chemical weapons. We are partly responsible for their suffering.

The Iran problem can be solved. The U.S. leadership must at long last change its ways and sit down at the negotiating table with the Iranian leadership—for top-level bilateral talks, or talks within the framework of a Middle East CSCE. It must offer Iran substantive security guarantees—as it did in the case of North Korea and ultimately Libya as well—in exchange for substantial concessions on its nuclear program and a verifiable commitment not to meddle in any way in the internal affairs of Iraq.

It is not just Iran's purported nuclear designs but also the very real nuclear weapons of today's nuclear powers that should be relegated to the junkyard of history. All nuclear weapons, including those of the United States, are—as the political hawk Ronald Reagan stated way back in 1986—"totally irrational, totally inhumane, good for nothing but killing, possibly destructive of life on earth and civilization." [167]

In 2007 even Henry Kissinger voiced support for such a "bold vision of a nuclear-free world." [168] The Nuclear Non-Proliferation Treaty calls in unequivocal terms for complete nuclear disarmament. The current nuclear powers are therefore all in permanent breach of the treaty. [169]

"Appeasement" does not represent the greatest danger of our time; it is the patriotic Western armchair strategists who cling obstinately to their narrow-minded view of the world and to their furtive racism, and who are letting the world slide into the same kind of foolhardy cycle of violence and counter-violence that led to the First World War.

Statesmanship instead of warfare: vigilant, patient and tenacious negotiations—that is the appropriate strategy towards the Muslim world, as it was in the East-West conflict. In a just world order, terrorism will find no sustenance and will fail to thrive.

In a nutshell, we must demonstrate both severity and justice—severity toward terrorism, and justice toward the Muslim world.

The objective must be a world order that all states can accept as just; a world in which there is no longer discrimination against Muslims in the West and against Jews and Christians in the Muslim world; a world which disarms the West's weapons of mass destruction and its lie machines; a world in which the U.S. is again admired as a symbol of peace and freedom, rather than of war and repression. A world in which everyone sees the log in his own eye and not only the speck in the eye of his neighbor.

Endnotes: Introduction

1   See: Mideast & N. Africa Encyclopedia: Bizerte Crisis (1961), quoted from: www.answers.
    com/topic/bizerte-crisis

2   Büchmann, Georg: *Geflügelte Worte. Der Citatenschatz des Deutschen Volkes (Winged Words. The
    Citatenschatz of the German People)*. Berlin 1898, digitized by Lars Aronsson, Linköping.

3   Eland, Ivan; Lee, Daniel: The Rogue State Doctrine and National Missile Defense, Foreign
    Policy Briefing 65, *Cato Institute*, March 29, 2001, www.cato.org/pubs/fpbriefs/fpb65.pdf

4   Whitlock, Craig: Al-Qaeda Branch Claims Algeria Blasts. Dozens Die in Strikes on Premier's
    Office, Police Post; 'New Front' Seen in N. Africa. *Washington Post*, April 12, 2007, p. A01,
    www.washingtonpost.com/wp-dyn/content/article/2007/04/11/AR2007041100371.html

Endnotes: Main Text

1   Jamail, Dahr, op. cit.: "If [the] U.S. leaves Iraq, the violent sectarianism between the Sunni and
    Shia will worsen. This is what Republicans and Democrats alike will have us believe. This key
    piece of rhetoric is used to justify the continuance of the occupation of Iraq."

2   In partial contradiction to the point of view of my conversational partner: Baker-Hamilton
    Report (2006), p. 18: "Leading Kurdish politicians [...] preferred to be within a democratic,
    federal Iraqi state because an independent Kurdistan would be surrounded by hostile neigh-
    bors. However, a majority of Kurds favor independence."

3   Qassim, Abdul-Zahraim: Famous Shi'ite Shrine in Samarra Attacked. *Infowars.com*, June
    13, 2007, http://infowars.com/articles/iraq/shrine_bombing_shiite_shrine_in_samarra_at
    tacked.htm. See also: unnamed author, Al-Maliki accuses security of involvement in mosque
    attack. *Middle East News*, by DPA, June 14, 2007.

4   Knickmeyer, Ellen; Finer, Jonathan: Insurgent Leader Al-Zarqawi Killed in Iraq. *Washington
    Post*, June 8, 2006, http://www.washingtonpost.com/wp-dyn/content/article/2006/06/08/
    AR2006060800114.html

5   Rioux, Jean-Pierre: *La Torture*, p.95. In: Rioux, Jean-Pierre; Gervereaux, Laurent: La France
    en guerre d'Algérie. Collection des publications de la Bibliothèque de documentation inter-
    nationale contemporaine. 1992, p. 92–99.

6   Tyson, Ann Scott: A Deadly Clash at Donkey Island. On a Routine Night Patrol Near Ramadi,
    U.S. Troops Stumble Upon a Camp of Heavily Armed Insurgents Poised to Retake the City.
    Washington Post, August 19, 2007, p. A01.

7   Enders, David: Camp Bucca: Iraq's Guantánamo Bay. *The Nation*, October 8, 2008, http://www.
    thenation.com/doc/20081027/enders: "[...] Camp Bucca, which in August held about 18,000
    detainees. Near the Kuwaiti border, Bucca shimmers in the predawn of the southern Iraqi des-
    ert, a beacon of light in a country where electricity is on for no more than twelve hours a day. It
    is the US military's largest detention center in Iraq. The total number of those officially in US
    custody in Iraq has fluctuated between a low of 7,200 and more than 26,000 since 2005."

8   Chew, Huibin Amee: Women and War: Reclaiming a Feminist Perspective. *Leftturn*, June 16,
    2007, www.leftturn.org/?q=node/699: "[...] according to Iraqi MP Mohamed al-Dainey, there
    were 65 documented cases of women's rape in occupation detention centers during 2006."

9   Shumway, Chris: Abu Ghraib General says she was told to treat Iraqis 'like dogs.' *The New Standard*, June 15, 2004, http://209.85.129.104/search?q=cache:GS9UU57EaX0J:newstanda rdnews.net/content/%3Faction%3Dshow_item%26itemid%3D551+geoffrey+miller+treat& hl=de&ct=clnk&cd=1&gl=de.

10 Unnamed author: Iraq celebrates football victory. *BBC News*, July 29, 2007, http://news.bbc. co.uk/2/hi/middle_east/6921078.stm

11 Wojcik, John: Iraq Inc. *People's Weekly World*, July 27, 2007, p. 10: "The State and Defense departments released figures July 4 that admit to more than 180,000 U.S. civilians working in Iraq under U.S. contracts. That figure, which exceeds by at least 20,000 the number of combat troops [...] does not include tens of thousands who have been hired by many of these as 'subcontractors' or tens of thousands who have been hired as 'private security.' [...] Military experts say that the United States has never in its history relied so heavily on private corporations to fight its wars. The Pentagon [...] says that the independent contractors do construction work, weapons systems maintenance and 'private security.' "

12 See: Afterword Endnote 81.

13 Salman, Raheem; Kennedy, J. Michael: In Cold Blood: Iraqi Tells of Massacre at Farmhouse. *Los Angeles Times*, July 6, 2006, p. A-1, http://articles.latimes.com/2006/jul/06/world/fg-rape6

14 Zoroya, Gregg: If Ramadi falls, 'province goes to hell.' *USA Today*, July 11, 2004, www.usato-day.com/news/world/iraq/2004-07-11-ramadi-usat_x.htm

15 Every day 17 former soldier kill themselves. Unnamed author: Suicide Epidemic Among Veterans. *CBS News*, November 13, 2007, www.cbsnews.com/stories/2007/11/13/cbsnews_ investigates/main3496471.shtml

16 A Dark Side to Iraq 'Awakening' Groups. *International Herald Tribune*, January 4, 2008: "Colonel Martin Stanton, chief of reconciliation and engagement for the Multinational Corps-Iraq, said [...]: 'These were people who last year were being hammered from two different directions: by Al-Qaeda and by us. It was probably a distasteful choice to make back then because, after all, they viewed us as invaders, and they probably still do, but it was a survival choice and they made it.' "

17 Beeston, Richard: Al-Qaeda targets tribes in Baghdad hotel. *Times Online*, June 25, 2007, www.timesonline.co.uk/tol/news/world/iraq/article1984885.ece

18 The U.S. war killed 655,000 Iraqis. "From the total number of war deaths approximately 600,000 people died through violence like shootings, car bombs and other explosions as well as air attacks. An estimated 31% or 186,000 deaths are, according to the study [*The Lancet*, see source below], attributed to the coalition forces—i.e., they were killed directly by the American military or their allies, According to the study 46% of the victims of violence died from bullet wounds—an unusually high number that refers to the immediate participation of the US military. Another 24% of the war related deaths are caused by other circumstances, i.e. ethnic or religious fighting and suicide attacks. In 45% of the cases the specific circumstances of death could not be determined." See also: Burnham, Gilbert. Mortality after the 2003 invasion of Iraq: a cross sectional cluster sample survey. *The Lancet*, October 11, 2006, available at http://www.brusselstribunal.org/pdf/lancet111006.pdf

19 Evans, Thomas; Keyes, Charley; Tawfeeq, Mohammed: Tribal leader: Evicting Iranian regime is only solution for Iraq. *CNN.com*, November 23, 2007, www.cnn.com/2007/WORLD/ meast/11/23/iraq.iran/: "Sheik Jasim al-Kadhim, president of the Association of Nationalist and Independent Iraqi Tribes from the south, condemned what he called Iran's meddling in Iraq by those affiliated with Quds Force, an arm of the Iranian Revolutionary Guard."

20 Lynch, Marc: What Iraqis Think, Again. *Global Policy Forum*, September 12, 2007, www. globalpolicy.org/security/issues/ iraq/poll/2007/0911iraqisthink.htm: "The BBC/ABC/NHK

survey, conducted in all 19 provinces during August [2007], finds that [...] 79% oppose the presence of Coalition forces in Iraq. 72% say that the presence of US forces is making security worse. When should US forces leave? 47% say 'leave immediately'—by far the highest support for immediate departure on record (it was 35% in February). 34% say stay until security is restored, 10% say stay until the Iraqi government is stronger. Only 2% say 'remain longer but leave eventually.' Only 1% of Sunnis say they have confidence in American forces. [...] Only 1% of Sunnis support the American presence in Iraq. Only 1% of Sunnis say that security has improved in Iraq as a whole in the last 6 months. 72% of Sunnis say that the US forces should leave immediately. 95% of Sunnis say that the presence of US troops makes security worse. 93% still see attacks on coalition forces as acceptable." www.globalpolicy.org/security/issues/iraq/resist/2007/09bbciraqipoll.pdf. Moreover in January 2008: Jamail, Dahr, op. cit.: "Will Iraq descend further into a sectarian nightmare if the occupation ends? An indicator [...] may be drawn from the southern city of Basra. In early September, 500 British troops left one of Saddam Hussein's palaces in the heart of the city and ceased to conduct regular foot patrols. According to the British military, the overall level of violence in the city has decreased 90 percent since then."

21 Gulf wars: 1980–1988 between Iraq and Iran; January 17, 1991–February 28, 1991 between Iraq and the allied armed forces under U.S. leadership; since March 20, 2003 between Iraq and the allied armed forces under U.S. leadership.

Endnotes: Afterword

1 For details of books cited in these endnotes please refer to the bibliography.

2 Olivier Le Cour Grandmaison, French historian. His main research covers French colonial history and French immigration politics.

3 François Maspero, French publicist and publisher.

4 Riedle, Gabriele: Die Pioniere Gottes (The Pioneers of God). *Geo*, February 1, 2007, p. 82.

5 Schaller, Christian: Völkerrechtliche Rahmenbedingungen und die Rolle der Vereinten Nationen bei der Terrorismusbekämpfung (International law basic conditions and the role of the United Nations during counterterrorism). In: Schneckener, Ulrich (Editor): Chancen und Grenzen multilateraler Terrorismusbekämpfung. Sammelstudie: Diskussionspapier FG 8, Nr. 7, June 2007. *Stiftung Wissenschaft und Politik*, Berlin, www.Swpberlin.org/de/common/get_document.php?asset_id=4129&PHPSESSID=2e7c6242ee1e349d9ae5be63aeb8ce a0: "Der andauernde Streit um die Definition von Terrorismus [...]. Die erste Kontroverse betrifft im Kern die Grenzziehung zwischen terroristischen Aktenauf der einen und legitimen gewaltsamen Handlungen zur Ausübungdes Selbstbestimmungsrechts der Völker auf der anderen Seite. [...]Die zweite Debatte wird darüber geführt, ob Maßnahmen staatlicher-Streitkräfte ebenfalls einen terroristischen Akt darstellen können oderob solche Handlungen vom Anwendungsbereich einer Terrorismus-Definition ausgeschlossen sein sollen. [...] 1994 verabschiedete die Generalversammlung eine Erklärung über Maßnahmen zur Beseitigung des internationalen Terrorismus, die erstmals Elementeeiner Terrorismus-Definition enthält. [...] Sie geht davon aus, dass kriminelle Akte, die darauf abzielen, zu politischen Zwecken einen Zustand des Terrors in der allgemeinen Öffentlichkeit oder innerhalb bestimmter Personengruppen zu verbreiten, weder aus politischen, philosophischen, ideologischen, rassischen, ethischen und religiösen noch aus sonstigen Gründen gerechtfertigt sind. Diese Formel macht deutlich, dass selbst dem Kampf zur Verwirklichung des Selbstbestimmungsrechts klare Grenzen gezogen sind."

Schirmer, Gregor: Befreiungskampf oder Terrorismus? *AG Friedensforschung an der Uni Kassel*, March 16, 2005, www.uni-kassel.de: "Es gibt bislang nur Ansätze einer allgemein anerkannten, völkerrechtlich verbindlichen Definition des internationalen Terrorismus. Das Zustandekommen des seit 1996 in den UN debattierten Entwurfs eines umfassenden Übereinkommens über den internationalen Terrorismus ist bisher gescheitert, weil die Staaten sich nicht über eine Definition verständigen konnten. Der Hauptstreitpunkt war von Anfang an und ist noch heute, den Befreiungskampf eindeutig vom Terrorismus zu unterscheiden und den Staatsterrorismus durch staatliche Streitkräfte von der Definition nicht auszuschließen, sondern mitzuerfassen. [...] Ein entscheidendes Kriterium der Abgrenzung legitimen Widerstands vom Terrorismus besteht darin, dass der Widerstandskämpfer seine bewaffneten Angriffe gegen die bewaffneten Kräfte der Besatzer und deren einheimische bewaffnete Handlanger richtet, aber nicht gegen Zivilisten, seien es Iraker oder Ausländer."

Payne, Caroll: Understanding Terrorism—Definition of Terrorism. *World Conflict Quarterly*, May 2007, http://www.globalterrorism101.com/UTDefinition.html: "The United States has defined terrorism under the Federal Criminal Code. Chapter 113B of Part I of Title 18 of the United States Code defines terrorism and lists the crimes associated with terrorism. In Section 2331 of Chapter 113b, terrorism is defined as: '... activities that involve violent ...' or life-threatening acts '... that are a violation of the criminal laws of the United States or of any State and ... appear to be intended (i) to intimidate or coerce a civilian population; (ii) to influence the policy of a government by intimidation or coercion; or (iii) to affect the conduct of a government by mass destruction, assassination, or kidnapping; and ..., if domestic '... (C) occur primarily within the territorial jurisdiction of the United States ..., if international '... (C) occur primarily outside the territorial jurisdiction of the United States ...'"

6   Unnamed author: Hezbollah Leader Hassan Nasrallah Talks With Former US Diplomats on Israel, Prisoners and Hezbollah's Founding. *Democracy Now*, July 28, 2006, http://www. democracynow.org/article.pl?sid=06/07/28/1440244#transcript: "In 1985, when I [Edward Peck] was the Deputy Director of the Reagan White House Task Force on Terrorism, [...] they asked us to come up with a definition of terrorism [...]. We produced about six, and each and every case, they were rejected, because careful reading would indicate that our own country had been involved in some of those activities. [...] you can read the U.S. definition of terrorism. And [...] one of the terms, 'international terrorism,' means 'activities that,' I quote, 'appear to be intended to affect the conduct of a government by mass destruction, assassination or kidnapping.' [...] you can think of a number of countries that have been involved in such activities. Ours is one of them. Israel is another. And so, the terrorist, of course, is in the eye of the beholder. [...] it's useful for people who discuss that phrase to remember that Israel was founded by terrorist organizations and terrorist leaders, Menachem Begin, who became statesmen and went on to win the Nobel Peace Prize."

7   Riedle, Gabriele (2007), p. 82.

8   Alexis de Tocqueville, French historian and politician. Between 1839 and 1848 Tocqueville belonged as a delegate to the moderate opposition. As a delegate he did two extensive travels to Algeria. He wrote several commission reports for the National delegation and several speeches with the settled conviction, Algeria should be a French colony with the "whites" occupying and the aborigines as non-equal servants.

      For more of Tocqueville's writing about Algeria: Pitts, Jennifer (Editor): Alexis de Tocqueville. *Writings on Empire and Slavery*. Baltimore (2001).

9   Alexis de Tocqueville, cited at www.mehr-freiheit.de/idee/tocqueville.html

10   Tocqueville, Alexis de: *Democracy in America*, Kramnick, Isaac; Bevan, Gerald, London 2003, p 371: "Among these very different men, the first to attract attention, the best educated, the most powerful, the happiest, is the white man, the European, the epitome of man; in a position inferior to him appear the Negro and the Indian." [Translation]

11 Tocqueville, Alexis de: Rapport sur le projet de loi relatif aux crédits extraordinaires demandés pour l'Algérie. In: Œvres. Paris.

12 C.f. Le Cour Grandmaison (2005), p. 90.

13 C.f. Maspero (1993), p. 319.

14 C.f. Le Cour Grandmaison (2005), p. 146–152.

15 C.f. Maspero (1993), p. 243; See also: Le Cour Grandmaison (2005), p. 141.

16 Lucien François de Montagnac, 1803–1845, French officer during the conquest of Algeria.

17 Colonel de Montagnac: Lettres d'un soldat. 1885. Cited after Maspero (1993), p. 193: "'On tue, on égorge; les cris des épouvantés, des mourants se mêlent au bruit des bestiaux qui mugissent […].' 'Vous me demandez ce que nous faisons des femmes que nous prenons. On en garde quelquesunes comme otages, les autres sont échangées contre des chevaux, et le reste est vendu, à l'enchère, comme bêtes de somme … Parmi ces femmes, il y en a souvent de très jolies.'"

See also: Zerrouky, Hassane: France-Algérie. Le crime avait un nom: le colonialisme. L'Humanité, June 17, 2000, www. survivreausida.net/a3175

18 Kelkel, Abdelkadar: Si c'est pour le rôle positif, nous avions déjà payé juillet 1830. Le Quotidien d'Oran, January 3, 2006, cited after www.algeria-watch.de/fr/article/pol/france/juillet_1830.htm: "Dans ses 'Lettres d'un soldat,' Montagnac, inhumain, relatant ses faits de guerre, avouait: 'Pour chasser les idées noires qui m'assiègent quel quefois, je fais couper des têtes. Non pas des têtes d'artichauts, mais des têtes d'hommes.'"

19 Louis de Baudicour, 1815–1883.

20 de Baudicour, Louis (1860): Histoire de la colonisation de l'Algérie. 1860, cited from Maspero (1993), p. 312: "Ici un soldat amputait, en plaisantant, le sein d'une pauvre femme […]; là un autre soldat prenait par les jambes un petit enfant et lui brisait la cervelle contre la muraille."

21 Hugo, Victor: Choses vues 1830–1848. Paris 1997, p. 168, cited from Le Cour Grandmaison (2005), p. 98, footnote 1: "Hugo connaît les atrocités commises par l'armée d'Afrique. 'Algérie, notet—il le 15 octobre 1852, le général Le Flô me disait hier soir que, dans les razzias, il n'était pas rare de voir des soldats jeter à leurs camarades des enfants qu'ils recevaient sur la pointe de leurs baïonnettes.'"

22 Le Cour Grandmaison (2005), p. 169, footnote 2: "Le Sémaphore marseillais, 2 mars 1833, cité par Bannister, Appel en faveur d'Alger et de l'Afrique du Nord par un Anglais, Paris, Dondey-Dupré, 1833, p. 26. 'Le noir animal,' appelé aussi 'charbon animal, est un charbon d'os que l'on obtient en calcinant les os en vase clos.' Utilisé dans l'industrie, 'pour la décoloration des liquides organiques et la réduction de certains oxydes,' il fut aussi employé pour la 'fabrication de sucre.'"

See also: D'Hérisson, Maurice: La Chasse à l'homme—Guerres d'Algérie, 1891: "'Nous rapportons un plein baril d'oreilles récoltées paire à paire sur les prisonniers, amis ou ennemis. […] Deux pieces de cent sous ne sont pas à dédaigner.' Journal d'un officier du corps expéditionnaire." Cited after: Unnamed author: Colonialisme. Le fardeau de l'homme blanc. L'Humanité, November 10, 2001, www.humanite.fr/Colonialisme-Le-fardeau-de-l-homme-blanc

See also: Maspero (1993), p. 186: "[…] il institue une prime à la tête coupée. Rapporter une tête c'est encombrant, mais il est quand meme plus facile d'en vérifier la provenance que lorsqu'il s'agit simplement de paires d'oreilles, dont un Yûsuf et un Montagnac se flattaient d'avoir rempli de pleins tonneaux. (Des oreilles, on peut en couper sur n'importe qui: la légende, rapportée par le comte d'Hérisson, veut que parmi les huit cents paires d'oreilles dûment salées—à cent sous chacune—que contenait l'un de ces tonneaux, on ait glissé celle d'un gendarme mort de la dysenterie.)"

23 See: Maspero (1993), p. 400: "[Napoléon III:] Or, si la France est maîtresse de L'Algérie, c'est que Dieu l'a voulu, et la nation ne renoncera jamais à cette conquête."

24 Ruscio, Alain; McGiffen, Steve (Transl.): A colonialist offensive and the "benefits" of colonialism. *L'Humanité in English*, December 16, 2005, www.humaniteinenglish.com/article17.html

25 Chelala, César: Meanwhile: The French Connection in the Export of Torture. *International Herald Tribune*, June 22, 2001, www.iht.com/articles/2001/06/22/edchel_ed3_php

26 Rioux, Jean-Pierre (1992), p. 99: "'Comment condamner les excès de la répression si l'on ignore ou l'on tait les débordements de la rébellion? [...]' écrivait Albert Camus le 10 janvier 1956."

27 The number of victims according to French estimates are between 1 and 1.5 million, according to Algerian estimates between 2.2 million Algerians and nearly 100,000 French. The numbers can be determined with the following sources:

    Unnamed author: Frankreich zeigt Algerien Position von Landminen. *Dimadima.de*, www.dimadima.de/modules.php?name=News&file=article&thold=-1&mode=flat&order=0&sid=574, 22.10.2007; Kateb, Kamel: Européen, Indigènes et Juifs en Algérie (1830–1962), Paris, Editions de l'Institut National d'Etudes Démographiques, 2001, p. 386; Girardet, Raoul: Without title. *La Revue L'Histoire*, Paris, 140, January 1991, p. 107.

28 Hayden, Tom: Ding dong; Tötet Saddam—ein Sommerhit? *Süddeutsche Zeitung*, August 7, 2003, p. 13.

29 Rogers, K.: We can't disregard the facts of history. *Hull Daily Mail*, April 23, 2003, p. 8, Letters. Macintyre, Ben: Invasion, bombs, gas—we've been here before. *The Times* (London), February 15, 2003. p. 20.

    Omissi, David: British bombing when the natives were restless. *Guardian Weekly*, February 3, 1991, p. 21.

30 Macintyre, Ben, p. 20 [cited Harris]: "'The Arab and Kurd now know what real bombing means, in casualties and damage: they know that within 45 minutes a fullsized village can be practically wiped out and a third of its inhabitants killed or injured,' he bragged."

31 Cockburn, Alexander: The press and the 'just war.' Persian Gulf War; Beat the Devil. *The Nation*, February 18, 1991, p. 6.

    See also: Omissi, David, p. 21.

32 Lionel Evelyn Oswald Charlton, 1879–1958, Officer in the Headquarters of the RAF Iraq-command 1923

33 Omissi, David, p. 21.

34 C.f. Libya: The Italian Occupation and the Libyan Resistance, http://ourworld.compuserve.com/hompages/dr_ibrahim_ighneiwa/re

35 Eckert, Andreas: Ordnung durch Terror. *Frankfurter Allgemeine Zeitung*, July 27, 2007, p. 8.

36 Gustave Le Bon, 1848–1931, French doctor and sociologist. See: http://www.gustave-le-bon.com/

37 Le Bon, Gustave (1889): Lois psychologiques de l'évolution des peuples. Paris 1978, p. 28, cited in Le Cour Grandmaison (2005), p. 81: "Dans la taxinomie raciale établie par Le Bon, par exemple, on découvre quatre races: les 'primitives,' où se trouvent 'les Fuégiens et les Australiens'; les 'inférieures,' représentées par les 'nègres'; les 'moyennes,' qui ont été capables de bâtir des civilisations importantes—les Chinois, les Mongols et les Arabes en font partie; et les supérieures, incarnées par les 'peuples indo-européens [...].'"

38 Fanon, Frantz: *The Wretched of the Earth*. New York (2005), p. 1 "... orders are given to reduce the inhabitants of the occupied territory to the level of a superior ape in order to justify the colonist's treatment of them as beasts of burden. Colonial violence not only aims at keeping ..."

39   Unnamed author: Iraq embargo scored, papal visit suggested. *Catholic World News* June 15, 1998, www.cwnews.com/news/viewstory.cfm?recnum=7860

See also: Unnamed author: Pope denounces sanctions on Iraq. Iraq-Vatican. *Politics*, March 20, 2000, www.arabicnews.com/ansub/Daily/Day/000320/2000032036.html

40   For a discussion about the statistics of victims see: Mahajan, Rahul: "We think the price is worth it." Media uncurious about Iraq policy's effects—there or here. *Fairness & Accuracy In Reporting* (FAIR), November/December 2001, www.fair.org

See also: Welch, Matt: The Politics of Dead Children. Have sanctions against Iraq murdered millions? *Reason*, March 2002, www.reason.com

See also: Unnamed author: Human costs of the 1991 Gulf war and sanctions on Iraq. *No War on Iraq*, Fact sheet 3, www.womenforpeace.org.au/FactSheet3vpn.pdf

41   See: Smallman, Lawrence: Iraq's real WMD crime. *Aljazeera.net*, January 9, 2005, www.al-jazeera.net

42   See: Main Text Endnote 18.

43   Differences in the assesment methods and partly also political interests result in a wide range of widely differing numbers of victims in Iraq. Also, the selection of more or less dangerous regions, independency or acceptance of the reporting institutions play an important role in the readiness to name and receive real figures. An assesment by the Iraqi health ministry, which is controlled by Muqtada al-Sadr, has to be regarded differently than an assessment from an independent institution. Figures and sources:

Iraqi Ministry of Health (IFHS), published by WHO, 2007 http://content.nejm.org/cgi/content/full/NEJMsa0707782: 151,000 violent deaths, until June 2006.

The Lancet, 2006, (independent) www.thelancet.com/webfiles/images/journals/lancet/s0140 673606694919.pdf: 655,000, of which 601,000 were violently killed until June 2006.

Opinion Research Business (ORB), 2007, (independent) http://www.opinion.co.uk/Newsroom_details.aspx?NewsId=78: 1.2 million violently killed until fall 2006.

Iraq Body Count, www.iraqbodycount.org: 47,668; counts only those killed violently, whose death is reported by at least two sources.

44   Colvin, Marie: Saddam's victims left to suffer as henchmen prosper. *Sunday Times* (London), February 3, 2008, p. 25: "Up to 15,000 men, women and children are believed to have been shot and buried here [Hilla, Iraq] when Saddam unleashed the elite Republican Guard on his rebellious people in 1991 [...]"

45   Kofi Annan expresses this as follows: Unnamed author: Kofi Annan interview: *BBC News*, Special Reports, December 31, 2006, http://newsvote.bbc.co.uk/): "BBC: 'Was it a mistake? Some Iraqis say that life is worse than it was under a dictator.' Kofi Annan: 'I think they are right in the sense of the average Iraqi's life. If I were an average Iraqi obviously I would make the same comparison, that they had a dictator who was brutal but they had their streets, they could go out, their kids could go to school and come back home without a mother or father worrying, "Am I going to see my child again?"'"

In addition see: Unnamed author: Students, teachers, schools face deliberate attacks in conflict areas—UNESCO. *UN Newscenter*, November 8, 2007, www.un.org/apps/news/story.asp?NewsID=24596&Cr=education&Cr1=unesco: "The study by the United Nations Educational, Scientific and Cultural Organisation [...] catalogues a range of assaults on education. [...] Principal author Brendan O'Malley [...] offered stark statistics on the problem, saying that 280 academics have been killed in Iraq between the fall of Saddam Hussein in 2003 and April this year 'in a campaign of liquidation.' Iraq finds its education system 'virtually on the point of collapse' with only 30 percent of pupils attending school last year compared with 75 percent the previous academic year."

See also: Baker-Hamilton Report (2006), p. 21: "Despite the positive signs, many leading economic indicators are negative. [...]. Inflation is above 50 percent. Unemployment estimates range widely from 20 to 60 percent."

46   Gehriger, Urs; Rueb, Matthias: The Weekly Standard Exclusive: An interview with Gen. Petraeus from the Swiss weekly Weltwoche and the Frankfurter Allgemeine Zeitung. *WeeklyStandard. com*, December 22, 2007, www.weeklystandard.com/Content/PublicArticles/000/000/014/52 7ynguz.asp

47   Langer, Gary. Iraqis' Own Surge Assessment: Few See Security Gains. ABC News/BBC/ NHK National Survey of Iraq Finds Worsening Public Attitudes. http://abcnews.go.com/us/ Story?id=3571504&page=3

48   Some consider the Turkish occupation of Northern Cyprus in 1974 an exception. Unnamed author: UN Secretary General Kofi Annan has unveiled a revised UN plan for the reunification of Cyprus. *BBC.com*, March 29, 2003, http://news.bbc.co.uk/2/hi/europe/3577733.stm: "In 1983, the Turkish-held area declared itself the Turkish Republic of Northern Cyprus, and is recognised internationally only by Turkey."

Unnamed author: Biden wants end to Cyprus occupation. In: *ekathimerini.com*, September 1, 2008, http://www.ekathimerini.com/4dcgi/_w_articles_politics_0_09/012008_100007: "[Joe] Biden, chairman of the Senate's Foreign Relations Committee—who has referred to the Cyprus occupation as an 'anomaly'—told Kathimerini that Washington's relations with Ankara 'will be influenced by how the Cyprus problem is solved, namely by the full withdrawal of Turkey, and from how Greek and Turkish differences in the Aegean are settled.'"

Not to be disregarded: Unnamed author: Iran's island offices condemned. *BBC.com*, August 3, 2008, http://news.bbc.co.uk/go/pr/fr/-/2/hi/middle_east/7596339.stm: "Abu Musa and the Greater and Lesser Tunb islands are controlled by Iran but claimed by the United Arab Emirates (UAE) with broad Arab support. [...] Iran took control of the islands in 1971 when Britain granted independence to its Gulf protectorates."

49   C.f. Enzensberger, Magnus (2006), p. 31.

50   Library of Congress. Country Studies, http://memory.loc.gov/ammem/index.html: Algeria. Arabization, December 1993.

51   Ruscio, Alain; McGiffen, Steve (Transl.).

52   C.f. Maspero (1993), p. 438: "Tocqueville [...]: 'Autour de nous,e crivait-il alors, les lumières se sont éteintes. Nous avons rendu la société musulmane beaucoup plus misérable, plus désordonnée, plus ignorante et plus barbare qu'elle n'était avant de nous connaître.'"

53   In addition see: Perliger, Arie; Weinberg, Leonhard: Jewish Self-Defense and Terrorist Groups Prior to the Establishment of the State of Israel: Roots and Traditions. *Terrorismexperts.org*, no date, http://terrorismexperts.org/index.html: "Despite the broad-based terrorist activities carried out by the 'Etzel' against the British authorities in Palestine of the 1940's, the 'Etzel' was neither the most violent nor the most extreme Jewish nationalist group struggling for sovereignty. Moreover, it was not this group that laid the foundations for Jewish terrorism following statehood. This role is reserved for the 'Lehi' organization.

See also: Nicholas, Bethell: The Palestine Triangle: The Struggle between British, Jews, and the Arabs, 1935–48 (1979), p. 278: [Yitzhak Shamir] "There are those who say that to kill Martin (a British sergeant) is terrorism, but to attack an army camp is guerrilla warfare and to bomb civilians is professional warfare. But I think it is the same from the moral point of view. Is it better to drop an atomic bomb on a city than to kill a handful of persons? I don't think so. But nobody says that President Truman was a terrorist."

54   Unnamed author: A View of History. *The King David Shopping Arcade* [brochure of the King

David Hotel], Jerusalem, no date, p. 22: "In 1936 the British Army leased this south wing that was targeted by the Jewish underground movement, ETZEL, headed by Menachem Begin, in their campaign to drive the British out of Palestine. The bomb planted in the basement kitchen of the La Regence restaurant, in July 1946, tore the British Headquarters apart and killed 91 people."

55   Daniel, Hans: War einmal ein Revoluzzer... *Junge Welt*, August 17, 2007, p. 12.

56   Waldman, Amy: Masters of Suicide Bombing: Tamil Guerrillas of Sri Lanka. *New York Times*, January 14, 2003, http://query.nytimes.com/gst/fullpage.html?res=9E06E1DB1231F937A25 752C0A9659C8B63.

Gouverneur, Cédric: Die Tamil Tigers sind die erfolgreichste Widerstandsbewegung der Welt. *Le Monde Diplomatique*, February 14, 2004, www.monde-diplomatique.de

57   www.consilium.europa.eu/ueDocs/cms_Data/docs/pressdata/en/misc/95034.pdf

58   Mohammad Mossadegh, 1881–1967, Iranian prime minister 1951–1953.

59   Richter, Horst-Eberhard: Feindbild Islamismus. Das Böse als Vorwand zur Militarisierung der Politik. *AG Friedensforschung an der Uni Kassel*, February 13, 2005, www.uni-kassel.de

See also: Hermann, Rainer: Ein Brief an das Weiße Haus. *Frankfurter Allgemeine Zeitung*, May 15, 2006, p. 12: "1952 *Time* Magazine crowned Mossadegh 'Man of the Year.' [...] A zesty detail is that Ahmadinejad in his letter to the American president refers to 1953 as the start of the alienation between Tehran and Washington." [Translation]

60   Parker, Ned: Saddam sentenced to death by hanging for massacre. *Times Online*, November 5, 2006, www.timesonline.co.uk/tol/news/world/iraq/article625743.ece

61   Ilsemann, Siegesmund von: Der Emissär des Präsidenten. *Der Spiegel*, November 17, 2003, p. 138.

See also: Fisk, Robert: Tod ist Leben, Niederlage Sieg. *Aurora Magazin*, www.aurora-magazin. at/gesellschaft/fisk_niederl_frm.htm

62   Krech, Hans; Schwilk, Heimo: Ein Veto für Öl und Waffen. *Welt am Sonntag*, March 9, 2003, p. 10.

See also: Guhl, Armin: Der Tod kommt lautlos—die geheimen Giftwaffen des Saddam Hussein. *Weltwoche*, February 5, 1998, p. 6, as well as Rötzer, Florian: Der Irak, die USA und die Massenvernichtungswaffen. *Telepolis*, October 16, 2002, www.heise.de

See also: Unnamed author: Resolution 612 (1988), UN-Sicherheitsrat, May 9, 1988, www. un.org/Depts/dpa/repertoire/85-88_05.pdf: "Condemns vigorously the continued use of chemical weapons in the conflict between the Islamic Republic of Iran and Iraq contrary to the obligations under the Geneva Protocol; [...] Expects both sides to refrain from the future use of chemical weapons in accordance with their obligations under the Geneva protocol [...]."

63   Huntington, Samuel P.: *The Clash of Civilization and the Remaking of World Order* (1996), p. 51: "The West won the world not by the superiority of its ideas or values or religion (to which few members of other civilizations were converted) but rather by its superiority in applying organized violence. Westerners often forget this fact, non-Westerners never do."

64   Watzal, Ludwig: Wer freut sich hier worüber? *Freitag*, 41, October 5, 2001, www.freitag. de/2001/41/01411202.php

65   C.f. Fanon, Frantz: *The Wretched of the Earth*. New York 2005, p. iii: "The repressed rage, never managing to explode, goes round in circles and wreaks havoc on the oppressed themselves. In order to rid themselves of it they end up massacring each other, tribes battle one against the other since they cannot confront the real enemy—and you can count on colonial policy to fuel rivalries; ...the torrent of violence to sweep away all the barriers. ...This is the age of the boomerang, the third stage of violence: it flies right back at us, it strikes us and, once again, we have no idea what hit us."

66   Unnamed author: Transcript: Ahmadinejad Interview, Part 1, *CBS News*, September 20, 2007 [before his visit to the UN in New York]: "Many innocent people were killed there [World Trade Center]. [...] We obviously are very much against any terrorist action and any killing. [...] Usually you go to these sites to pay your respects. And also to perhaps air your views about the root causes of such incidents. I think that when I do that, I will be paying, as I said earlier, my respect to the American nation." [*60 Minutes* correspondent Scott Pelley interviewed Iranian President Mahmoud Ahmadinejad in Tehran.]

67   Encyclopaedia of the Orient, http://lexicorient.com/e.o/hamas.htm, Art. Hizbullah: "Lebanese Shi'i Muslim political group, often involved in military actions. [...]" See also: www.hagalil. com/israel/kibbutz/lexikon.htm, Art. Hisbollah (Arab.: Party of God): "Pro-Iranian Terror Organization in Lebanon."

68   Encyclopaedia of the Orient, http://lexicorient.com/e.o/hamas.htm, Art. Hamas: "Palestinian Islamist political group founded in 1987, involved in both social programs in the Palestinian territories, as well as military actions against Israel. [...]" See also: www.hagalil.com/israel/kib-butz/lexikon.htm, Art. Hamas: "(Arab.:Harakat al Muqawama al Islamiya). Islamic Resistance Movement, named for the radical Islamic terror group of the Palestinians. [...]."

69   Halaby, Jamal: Jordanians, others in Middle East, mourn U.S. Terrorist attack victims. *BC Cycle*, September 15, 2001.

       See also: Unnamed author: World unites in sympathy with grieving Americans. *The Record* (Kitchener-Waterloos, Ontario), September 15, 2001, p. A03.

70   Unnamed author: Iraq war illegal, says Annan. *BBC News Online*, April 16, 2004, http://news.bbc.co.uk/go/pr/fr/-/2/hi/middle_east/3661134.stm: "The United Nations Secretary-General Kofi Annan has told the BBC the US-led invasion of Iraq was an illegal act that contravened the UN charter."

       See also: Zumach, Andreas: Zur Stärkung des Völkerrechts und der Zivilcourage. Die Verleihung des Amos-Preises an Florian Pfaff, Major der Bundeswehr. Laudatio von Andreas Zumach, March 4, 2007. *Zeit-Fragen*, March 26, 2007, www.zeit-fragen.ch/index.php?id=1671: "The prize was given to [...] Bundeswehr (German Armed Forces) Major Florian Pfaff who refused to obey orders during the Iraq war. First, he was demoted, but later completely reinstated by the Federal Administrative Court. [...] Major Pfaff refused to follow the explicit, but outrageously unlawful orders of his military superiors to participate in the Iraq war of 2003. [...] Literally, the judgment reads: 'A state that for whatever reasons and without justification disregards the ban on violence of the UN Charter, and resorts to military force, acts against international law and commits military aggression.' Therefore the Anglo-American war of 2003 is clearly classified as violating international laws on warfare." [Translation]

       See also: www.bundesverwaltungsgericht.de/enid/daa0c45757482e98c9e4ab54ac54dc3,faf28 37365617263685f646973706c6179436f6e7461696e6572092d0935363933/Entscheidung ssuche/Entscheidungssuche_80.html

71   Ross, Jan: Wer einmal lügt, dem glaubt man nie wieder. Nur der Erfolg kann Bush/Blair im Irak noch Recht geben. *Die Zeit*, July 24, 2003, http://images.zeit.de/text/2003/31/01_leit_2

       See also: Strutynski, Peter: Von Lügen und anderen Peinlichkeiten. *AG Friedensforschung an der Uni Kassel*, June 14, 2003, http://www.uni-kassel.de/fb5/frieden/regionen/Irak/stru-kom-mentar.html

72   Harris, Whitney R.: The Crime Of Waging Aggressive War. An Address by Whitney R. Harris. Prosecutor at the Trial of the Major German War Criminals at Nuremberg and the Author of *Tyranny On Trial*. In: The Robert H. Jackson Center, October 1, 2004, www. roberthjackson.org/Man/SpeechesßAboutßWhitneyHarrißTyranny: "On the issue of aggressive war, the Tribunal declared: [...] 'To initiate a war of aggression, therefore, is not only an international crime; it isthe supreme international crime, differing only from other

crimes in that it contains within itself the accumulated evil of the whole.' "

73   Robert H. Jackson, 1892–1954. See: www.roberthjackson.org/Man/

74   Unnamed author: Pursuing Human Dignity: The Legacies of Nuremberg for International Law, Human Rights, and Education. In: Harvard Law School, 3–4. November 2005, www.law.harvard.edu/conferences/ nuremberg?legacies/: "We must never forget that the record on which we judge these defendants today is the record on which history will judge us tomorrow." See also: Taylor, Telford: *The Anatomy of the Nuremberg Trials: A Personal Memoir* (1993): "The laws of war do not apply only to the suspected criminals of vanquished nations. There is no moral or legal basis for immunizing victorious nations from scrutiny. The laws of war are not a one-way street."

75   Richter,Horst-Eberhard,www.uni-kassel.de/fb5/frieden/themen/Sicherheitskonferenz/2005-richter.html

76   http://web2.justiz.hessen.de/migration/rechtsp.nsf/4dd04a17de79c763c1257249004a7703/d b89ffcf48f74356c12570c30053cd0e?OpenDocument&Click=: "Premeditation: [...] After differentiating possible premeditation from deliberate negligence, especially considering common criteria of criminal law (c.f. Dreher-Tröndle, StGB, § 15, Rn. 84; Schönke-Schröder, StGB, § 15 Rn. 72 ffesp. Rn. 84) the difference is that in possible premeditation the person acting accepts the consequences and risks, therefore approves and takes risks and consequences into account; with deliberate negligence the person trusts that there is no evidence and no successful outcome of the deed [...] BVerwG, 18.09.2003–2 WD 3.03–1. Conditional premeditation is not only given when the perpetrator agrees with the possible successful outcome of his deed, either implied or explicit, but also when he accepts the unwanted, but necessary success for the sake of his goals."

77   See: Main Text Footnote p. 49.

78   See: Main Text Footnote p. 90.

79   Herding, Richard: "Die Zivilgesellschaft stärken." *TAZ*, July 28, 2003, p. 14. In addition: Schlötzer, Christiane: Kooperation umständehalber. *Süddeutsche Zeitung*, September 11, 2002, p. 10.

80   Meyer, J.; Vehlewald, H. J.: Ging es den Irakern unter Saddam besser? *Bild Online*, December 5, 2006, www.bild.t-online.de/BTO/news/aktuell/2006/12/05/irak-annan-saddam/irak-annan-saddam.html: "Jeden Tag verüben Terroristen 180 Angriffe, 2003 waren es nur acht."

81   Dobrow, Robert: U.S. escalation arouses greater popular resistance in Iraq. *Workers*, April 22, 2007, www.workers.org/2007/world/iraq-0426: "According to the Brookings Institution [Washington DC], 75 percent of all the recorded attacks in Iraq are directed at occupation forces, and a further 17 percent at Iraqi government forces. [...] A poll conducted last month for the BBC, ABC News, ARD German TV and *USA Today*, which got scant attention in the U.S. press, showed that the percentage of Iraqis who opposed the presence of U.S.-led forces in their country increased [...] to 78 percent in 2007."

      In addition: Childs, Nick: Iraq poll makes for grim reading. *BBC News*, September 10, 2007, http://news.bbc.co.uk/2/hi/middle_east/6986993.stm: "The poll, conducted in August, also indicates that Iraqi opinion is at its gloomiest since the BBC/ABC News polls began in February 2004. According to this latest poll, in key areas—security and the conditions for political dialogue, reconstruction and economic development—between 67 and 70% of Iraqis, or more than two-thirds, say the surge has made things worse. [...] 85% of Iraqis say they have little or no confidence in US and UK forces. [...] In terms of quality of life, 80% of Iraqis say the availability of jobs is bad or very bad, 93% say the same about electricity supplies, 75% for clean water, 92% for fuel. And 77% of Iraqis say the ability to live where they want, without persecution, is bad or very bad."

82 Wilson, Emily: "What Connors and Bingham discovered has been corroborated by Department of Defense reports, which found that over 70 percent of the attacks in Iraq from 2004 to 2007 targeted U.S.-led coalition forces, and by BBC/ABC polls, which said all the Iraqis polled disapprove of attacks on civilians, but the majority approve of attacks on the U.S. troops."

83 Zenz, Helmut: Das Leben des Mohammed. 2002. www.helmutzenz.de/hzisla10.html

84 Urban II, Pope (1088–99), called the occidental Christians to their first crusade in 1095. The expression "Deus lo vult—God wants it" resulted as a reaction from his listeners during his council homily in Clermont.

85 Follath, Erich et.al.: "Gott will es." *Der Spiegel*, October 8, 2001, p. 160.

86 Pernoud, Régine: Die Kreuzzüge in Augenzeugenberichten. Düsseldorf 1965, p. 97–102. www.stabi.hs-bremerhaven.de/gbs2/welt-jahrtausend/zeugen.htm

87 Küng, Hans (2005), p. 168.

88 Jeremiah 51:27: "Raise up battle flags throughout the lands.

Sound the trumpets calling the nations to do battle.

Prepare the nations to do battle against Babylonia.

Call for these kingdoms to attack her:

Ararat, Minni, and Ashkenaz.

Appoint a commander to lead the attack.

Send horses against her like a swarm of locusts

Jeremiah 51:28: "Prepare the nations to do battle against her.

Prepare the kings of the Medes.

Prepare their governors and all their leaders.

Prepare all the countries they rule to do battle against her."

See also: Aslan, Reza (2006), p. 102.

89 Rummel, Rudy: Maybe 50 Million Murdered in Colonial Democide. *H-Net Discussion Networks*, November 2, 2001, http://h-net.msu.edu/cgi-bin/logbrowse.pl?trx=vx&list=h gen ocide&month=0111&week=a&msg=Wb7FMT0fVR%2bRyAIUchE2DA&user=&pw=

90 Hall, Rod: Der nächste Weltkrieg kommt bestimmt. *Gute Nachrichten*, March 1999, www. gutenachrichten.org

See also: www.volksbund-hamburg.de/wir/zahlen.htm and Rummel, Rudolph J.: "Demozid" der befohlene Tod: Massenmorde im 20. Jahrhundert. Münster et al. 2006.

See also: www.shoa.de/content/section/2/46/

91 See: Sura 2:256: "There is no compulsion in religion. The right direction is henceforth distinct from error. And he who rejecteth false deities and believeth in Allah hath grasped a firm handhold which will never break. Allah is Hearer, Knower."

See also: Avnery, Uri; Rohlfs, Ellen (Transl.): Mohammeds Schwert. Der Papst, der Islam, die Gewalt und die Kreuzzüge. *Freace*, Sept. 25, 2006, www.freace.de

See also: Kiesel, Heiner (2006): Der Tag des friedlichen Zorns? *Frankfurter Allgemeine Zeitung*, September 19, 2006, p. 42: [Jussuf al-Qardawi, Fernsehprediger bei Al-Dschasira]: "The purpose of the Jihad, the 'Holy War' is self-defense and not to force Islam onto others. It is written in the Qur'an. There is no force in religion." [Translation]

See also: Amir Zaidan in a personal letter to the author: "It is a fact that never during Islamic history Muslims have forced Islam upon others. The statements of some Orientalists, that the Ottomans have kidnapped Christian children to educate them as Janissaries is an assumption only found in the writing of Western Orientalists. The Janissaries started as children; they came from Muslim and non-Muslim families that had become victims of the war. They were raised and educated as Muslims and knew only the Islamic way of life. They were loyal towards the sultan. We cannot speak of force for these people were not forced into anything new. On the other hand, we read in many Islamic works that some kalifs and sultans did not want too many people to convert to Islam. They were more important for the *Dschizya* tax (I translate it as "defense charge," Orientalists translate it as "head tax"). This Dschizya was no pressure to convert to Islam as some Orientalists say, for it was not paid by women, children or priests, but only by men who were able to fight. Islam freed these men from fighting with Muslims; therefore they had to pay a protection tax. At times, non-Muslims fought with Muslim against their enemies and were freed from the tax. The tax took into consideration the life circumstances of people. The poor paid 12 Dirham silver coins per year, those with medium income paid 24 Dirham, [and] the rich paid 48 Dirham." [Translation]

92 Hermann, Rainer: Kein Weg zum Dialog. Gegenüber den Armeniern hatten sich die Jungtürken für Repression und gegen Reformen entschieden. *Frankfurter Allgemeine Zeitung*, March 21, 2001, p. 16.

93 Schmitz, Thorsten: "Israel schöpft aus jeder Wunde Kraft." Interview with President Shimon Peres. *sueddeutsche.de*, January 1, 2008, www.sueddeutsche.de/ausland/artikel/703/150332/: "The Palestinians and Islam are no enemies. We do not fight against the Palestinians or their religion. We have the same parents, Abraham and Moses."

See also: Bartezko, Dieter: Wir sind Kinder des Orients. Homers Geheimnis. *FAZ.NET*, December 29, 2007, www.faz.net/s/Rub117C535CDF414415BB243B181B8B60AE/Doc~E9C44A2B51D6C47F18BAAC295393CF8B1~ATpl~Ecommon~Scontent.html?rss_feuilleton: "The *Iliad* appears as a possibly common work of such ostensibly different cultures. With Raoul Schrott's Homer [...] facts of common roots are evident. If they make their way from science into politics and the general consciousness of Occident and Orient they might lead to mutual respect." [Translation]

94 Numbers 31:7, 15, 17: "They fought against the Midianites, as the Lord commanded Moses, and they killed every male." "Moses said to them, "Have you allowed all the women to live? Now therefore kill every boy, and kill every woman who has had sexual intercourse with a man."

95 Matthew 10:34: "Do not think that I have come to bring peace to the earth. I have not come to bring peace but a sword."

96 Luther, Martin: Tischgespräche. Cited from: Vinnai, Gerhard: *Jesus und Ödipus*. Frankfurt (1999), p. 175, cited from Deschner, Karlheinz: *Abermals krähte der Hahn*. Stuttgart (1971), p. 484.

97 Surah 4:89: "They long that ye should disbelieve even as they disbelieve, that ye may be upon a level (with them). So choose not friends from them till they forsake their homes in the way of Allah; if they turn back (to enmity) then take them and kill them wherever ye find them, and choose no friend nor helper from among them."

98 Leviticus 19:18: "You must not take vengeance or bear a grudge against the children of your people, but you must love your neighbor as yourself. I am the Lord."

99 Matthew 5:6: "Blessed are those who hunger and thirst for righteousness, for they will be satisfied." 5:10 "Blessed are those who are persecuted for righteousness, for the kingdom of heaven belongs to them." The second is like it: 22:39: "Love your neighbor as yourself."

100 Surah 4:36: "And serve Allah. Ascribe no thing as partner unto Him. (Show) kindness unto parents, and unto near kindred, and orphans, and the needy, and unto the neighbor who is of kin (unto you) and the neighbor who is not of kin, and the fellow-traveller and the wayfarer and (the

slaves) whom your right hands possess. Lo! Allah loveth not such as are proud and boastful."

See also: "A word you and we have in common." Open letter and appeal of (138) Muslim religious leaders to His Holiness Pope Benedict XVI, October 13, 2007, www.acommonword.com.

101 C.f. http://dreifaltigkeit-altdorf.de/zehn_gebote.htm and Krausen, Helma: Was der Koran zum Judentum sagt. *Talmud.de*, December 20, 2007, www.talmud.de/cms/Was_sagt_der_ Koran_zum_Ju.39.0.html: "In the meccan sections of the Qur'an we find general principles on faith and ethics with an emphasis on individual responsibility, including the concentrated section in Surah 17:22–38 that shows clear parallels to biblical decalog."

102 Surah 50:38: "And verily We created the heavens and the earth, and all that is between them, in six Days, and naught of weariness touched Us."

See also: Schirrmacher, Christine. Die Eigenschaften Gottes im Koran und Islam. *Internetarchiv des Lutherischen Konvents im Rheinland*, www.ekir.de/lutherkonvent/archiv/schirrm1.html

103 Küng (2005), p. 161.

104 Cited and agreed after a personal conversation with the author. Since 1996 Zakzouk is minister for religious affairs and president of the highest Islamic coucil in Egypt.

105 Surah 29:46: "And argue not with the People of the Scripture unless it be in (a way) that is better, save with such of them as do wrong; and say: We believe in that which hath been revealed unto us and revealed unto you; our God and your God is One, and unto Him we surrender."

See also: Ein Wort das uns und euch gemeinsam ist. Offener Brief und Aufruf, in addition.: "[So] God affirms in the Holy Qur'an that the Prophet did not [say] anything fundamentally new.: 'Nothing else is said to you as has been told to you by the (Fussilat 41:43). Speak: I am no new inventor among the messengers. [...].' [...] As Muslims we tell Christians that we are not against them and that Islam is not against them. [...]." [Translation]

106 Unnamed author: Zusammenleben mit Muslimen in Deutschland. *Eine Handreichung des Rates der EKD*, 2000, www.ekd.de/glauben/islamß2000ßislam2.html

See also: op. cit. "A word you and we have in common."

107 Rummel, Rudolph J.: *Death by Government*. New Brunswick (1994), Table 1.4: This Century's Bloodiest Dictators. www.hawaii.edu/powerkills/NOTE1.HTM

108 Taheri, Ahmad: Unauffälliges Schreckenskabinett. *Frankfurter Allgemeine Zeitung*, August 23, 2006, p.3.

109 Harrison, Frances: Iran's proud but discreet Jews. *BBC News*, September 22, 2006, http:// news.bbc.co.uk/2/hi/middle_east/5367892.stm

110 Wright, Robin: *The Last Great Revolution: Turmoil and Transformation in Iran*, New York (2001), p. 207.

See also: Taheri, Ahmad, p. 3.

111 www.britannica.com: Cyrus II, King of Persia, a/k/a Cyrus the Great, born 590–580 BC, Media, or Persis [now in Iran] died c. 529, Asia. Conqueror who founded the Achaemenian empire, centered on Persia and comprising the Near East from the Aegean Sea eastward to the Indus River. He is also remembered in the Cyrus legend—first recorded by Xenophon, Greek soldier and author, in his *Cyropaedia*—as a tolerant and ideal monarch who was called the father of his people by the ancient Persians. In the Bible he is the liberator of the Jews who were captive in Babylonia.

See also: 2 Chronicles 36:22 In the first year of the reign of King Cyrus of Persia, in fulfillment of the promise he delivered through Jeremiah, the Lord moved King Cyrus of Persia to issue a written decree throughout his kingdom. It read: "This is what King Cyrus of Persia says: 'The Lord God of the heavens has given to me all the kingdoms of the earth. He has appointed me to build for him a temple in Jerusalem in Judah. May the Lord your God energize you who belong to his people, so you may be able to go back there!"

Isaiah 48:14–15: "All of you, gather together and listen! Who among them announced these things? The Lord's ally will carry out his desire against Babylon; he will exert his power against the Babylonians I, I have spoken—yes, I have summoned him; I lead him and he will succeed."

But: Quetteville, Harry de: Cyrus cylinder's ancient bill of rights 'is just propaganda.' In: *Telegraph.co.uk*, July 21, 2008: "The Cyrus cylinder, which is held by the British Museum, is a legacy of Cyrus the Great—the Persian emperor famed for freeing the Jews of ancient Babylon after conquering the city in 539 BC. A copy of the cylinder, which is covered in cuneiform script supposed to detail the ancient charter of rights, also hangs next to the Security Council Chamber in the United Nations headquarters in New York, where it is held as a symbol of Cyrus's reputation as a fair and just ruler. But now that reputation has been challenged by German historians who claim that the UN is unjustly celebrating the rule of a man every bit as despotic as any other land-grabbing leader."

112 Isaiah 45:1, 13: "This is what the Lord says to his chosen one, to Cyrus, whose right hand I hold in order to subdue nations before him, and disarm kings, to open doors before him, so gates remain unclosed: It is me—I stir him up and commission him; I will make all his ways level. He will rebuild my city; he will send my exiled people home, but not for a price or a bribe," says the Lord who commands armies."

Isaiah 48:14 f.: "Yahweh chose Cyrus: [...]. Who is loved by the Lord will execute Babel's will and bring about his will with the Chaldeans. I have spoken and I have called upon him/ I have let him come/ and he will complete his path."

113 For a summary of the discussion see *Guardian* columnist Jonathan Steele's commentary "Lost in translation," June 14, 2006, www.ifamericansonlyknew.com/us_ints/ir-steele.html: "The fact that he [Ahmadinejad] compared his desired option—the elimination of 'the regime occupying Jerusalem'—with the fall of the Shah's regime in Iran makes it crystal clear that he is talking about regime change, not the end of Israel."

See also: Bronner, Ethan: Just How Far Did They Go, Those Words Against Israel? *New York Times*, June 11, 2006, www.nytimes.com/2006/06/11/weekinreview/11bronner.html

114 Unnamed author: Iranische Abgeordnete rügen Brief-Diplomatie. *Netzeitung.de*, July 28, 2006, www.netzeitung.de/ausland/428185.html

115 Borgstede, Michael: Erst der Messias, dann der Staat, *FAZ:NET*, December 12, 2006, www.faz.net/s/RubB30ABD11B91F41C0BF2722C308D40318/Doc~EA8ED0E2055A64BD7A C9F51EA546075DD~ATpl~Ecommon~Scontent.html

See also: Avnery, Uri: Ein Krieg zwischen Religionen? Um Himmels Willen, nein! *Znet*, February 18, 2006, http://zmag.de/artikel/Ein-Kriegzwischen-Religionen-Um-Himmels-willen-nein

116 Harrison, Frances: "Anti-Semitism is not [...] an Islamic or Iranian phenomenon—anti-semitism is a European phenomenon, he says, arguing that Jews in Iran even in their worst days never suffered as much as they did in Europe."

117 Hoffmann, Andrea Claudia: Bombenstimmung. *Focus*, May 8, 2006, p. 206.

Motadel, David: Was der Brotpreis im Iran mit dem Atomprogramm zu tun hat. *Le Monde Diplomatique*, February 9, 2007. www.mondediplomatique.de/pm/2007/02/09.mondeText. artikel,a0034.idx,5

See also: Unnamed author: Iran: Alle Forderungen erfüllt. *Frankfurter Allgemeine Zeitung*, November 23, 2007, p. 8.

See also: Taheri, Ahmad: Schläge unter die Gürtellinie. *Frankfurter Allgemeine Zeitung*, November 28, 2007, p. 3.

118 Erck, Cristina: Ein bisschen Freiheit. *Focus*, June 18, 2001, p. 260.

See also: Hoffmann, Andrea Claudia: Gegenwind im Gottesstaat. *Focus*, December 22, 2006, p. 140.

119 Leixnering, Andreas: Verbunden in Abneigung: USA und Iran. *Deutsche Welle*, July 23, 2007, www.dw-world.de/dw/article/0,2144,2703867,00.html

120 Unnamed author: Ich bin verwundert. *Der Spiegel*, July 10, 2006, p. 17. Annette Schavan interview about her judicial defeat in the headscarf dispute.

121 Gelinsky, Katja: Zum Schutz der Frommen. Die einseitige Bürgerrechtspolitik der Bush-Regierung. *Frankfurter Allgemeine Zeitung*, July 20, 2007, p. 30.

122 Sezgin, Hilal: Schavans Hundeknochen. *Die Zeit*, July 13, 2006, p. 35.

123 Text collection with quotes by Mohammed (completed in the 9th and 10th centuries; next to the Qur'an an important source of religious rules).

124 Unnamed author: On Their Honor. *New York Times*, March 31, 1991, http://query.nytimes.com/gst/fullpage.html?res=9D0CEFDF123EF932A05750C0A967958260

See also: United Nations, General Assembly, Report of the Secretary-General, July 2, 2002, http://www.unhchr.ch/huridocda/huridoca.nsf/AllSymbols/985168F508EE799FC1256C520 02AE5A9/$File/N0246790.pdf

125 Metzke, Robert: Boosting the Female Side of Science: Germany Wants to Double the Number of Women Professors. *Science Magazine*, January 21, 2000, http://sciencecareers.sciencemag. org/career_development/previous_issues/articles/0280/boosting_the_female_side_of_science_germany_wants_to_double_the_number_of_women_professors

See also: Schmidt, Marion: Streitfall Frauenquote. *Süddeutsche Zeitung*, June 12, 2006, p. 18.

126 Unnamed author: More women pursuing university degrees in Iran. *Taipei Times*, November 5, 2006, p. 9, www.taipeitimes.com/News/editorials/archives/2006/11/05/2003334951

127 Kohler-Gehrig, Eleonora: Die Geschichte der Frauen im Recht. *Fach hoch schule Ludwigsburg Online-Dokumente: Frauen in der Geschichte*, August 2003, www.fh-ludwigsburg.de/service/ skripte/kohlergehrig/frauenimrecht.pdf: "On June 18, 1957 the law of equal rights became effective. [...] The power of man to end a service relationship between him and his wife was eliminated." [Translation]

See also: http://www.frauenportal.essen.de/index.htm?3gesedat.htm?3gesetz1.htm: Spektaku läre Änderungen des BGB im Jahre 1957.

128 Genesis 3:16: "To the woman he said,

'I will greatly increase your labor pains;

with pain you will give birth to children.

You will want to control your husband,

but he will dominate you.'"

1 Corinthians 14:34: "The women should be silent in the churches, for they are not permitted to speak. Rather, let them be in submission, as in fact the law says."

129 Ninth United Nations survey of crime trends and operations of criminal justice systems [...] 1–9. United Nations Office on drugs and crime: http://en.wikipedia.org/wiki/List_of_countries_by_murder_rate#2000s

130 C.f. Lessing, Gotthold Ephraim: Nathan der Weise (3. Akt, 7. Szene), Ringparabel (1779).

Lessing-Akademie.de, www.lessingakademie.de/ringparabel/ringparabel.html

131 Merkel, Angela: Speech by the German Chancellor in the European Parliament in Strassburg, January 17, 2007. *Die Bundeskanzlerin Online*, www.bundeskanzlerin.de/nn_5296/Content/DE/Rede/2007/01/2007-01-17-bkin-rede-ep.html

132 Unnamed author: [Frank] Graham clarifies comments on Islam. From *Journal Sentinel* wire reports. *The Milwaukee Journal Sentinel*. December 5, 2001: "Graham, the son of evangelist Billy Graham, was criticized by several groups for saying earlier that Islam 'is a very evil and wicked religion.'"

133 Cited from: Karim, Altaf: Kansas State University: Column: Death of objectivity in the news media. *U-Wire*, August 24, 2004: "[...] But on a June 17 broadcast [Fox News], O'Reilly said, '... And I don't have any respect, by and large, for the Iraqi people at all. I have no respect for them. I think that they're a prehistoric group that is ... yeah, ... we cannot intervene in the Muslim world ever again.

     'What we can do is bomb the living daylights out of them, just like we did in the Balkans.'"

134 Coulter, Ann: Muhammad Cartoons: Muslim Bites Dog. *Human Events Online*, February 15, 2006: "[...] Perhaps we could put aside our national, ongoing, post-9/11 Muslim butt-kissing contest and get on with the business at hand: Bombing Syria back to the stone age and then permanently disarming Iran."

     See also: Unnamed author: You may love her, you may hate her, but you won't ignore her. *Grand Rapids Press* (Michigan), February 17, 2006, p. A1: "Among the statements by political commentator Ann Coulter that have sparked controversy: [...] 'We should invade their countries, kill their leaders and convert them to Christianity.'—speaking of Arab terrorists, Sept. 2001."

135 Thomas, Gina: Das Gesetz des weißen England im Rassismus-Streit: Terry Eagleton attackiert Martin und Kingsley Amis. *Frankfurter Allgemeine Zeitung*, November 24, 2007, p. 37.

     See also: Stein, Hannes: Juden als Kronzeugen gegen das Judentum. *Welt Online*, October 23, 2007, www.welt.de

     See also: John, Robert: Israel—Dämonisierung als neue literarische Gattung. *Pickings.de*, o.J., www.pickings.de/tiki-view_blog_post.php?find=&blogId=11&offset=0&sort_mode=created_desc&postId=2528&show_comments=1, October 23, 2007.

     See also: Jörges, Hans-Ulrich: Nach Mohammed ... *Der Stern*, February 9, 2006, p. 60.

136 Amir, Eli: Die Furcht des Besatzers vor den Besetzten. Man kann von Europa lernen, dass Grenzen nicht heilig sind: Bemerkungen zum israelisch-palästinensischen Konflikt und die Möglichkeit seiner Überwindung. *Frankfurter Rundschau*, November 22, 2000.

     Current size of Muslim population in the Middle East, see e.g., CIA World Factbook.

137 Unnamed author: Raketenangriffe auf Israel. *Frankfurter Allgemeine Zeitung*, December 29, 2006, Current numbers at: B'TSELEM. Statistics. 2008, www.btselem.org/english/Statistics/Casualties.asp: Fatalities 29.9.2000–31.12.2007.

138 See: Afterword Endnote 93.

139 Le Cour Grandmaison (2005), p. 21, 211.

140 Cited from Weickmann, Dorion: Geschichtsmoral à la Grosser. *Süddeutsche Zeitung*, August 30, 2006, p. 12.

141 Johannes Gross: "Je länger das Dritte Reich zurückliegt, umsomehr nimmt der Widerstand gegen Hitler und die Seinen zu." Cited from Broder, Henryk M. Der programmierte Eklat. *Der Spiegel*, October 30, 2007, www.spiegel.de

142 About the scale of the costs of war there are numerous figures and estimates besides the offcial number, i.e.: Barrett, Ted; Brittain, Becky; Fabian, K.D.: War costs could total $1.6 trillion by 2009, panel estimates. *CNN.com*, November 14, 2007, http://edition.cnn.com/2007/POLITICS/11/13/hidden.war.costs/index.html: "The total economic impact of the wars in Iraq and Afghanistan is estimated at $1.6 trillion by 2009, a congressional committee said in a report released Tuesday."

Glantz, Aaron: Iraq, Afghanistan War costs Top Vietnam. *Antiwar.com*, December 21, 2007, www.antiwar.com/glantz/?articleid=12090: "According to a study by the Washington-based Center for Arms Control and Non-Proliferation, Congress has now approved nearly $700 billion for the wars in Iraq and Afghanistan. 'Using inflationadjusted dollars, the total cost of those wars has now surpassed the total cost of the Vietnam war (which ran to $670 billion),' the group's Travis Sharp told One World. 'It's also more than seven times larger than the Persian Gulf War ($94 billion) and more than twice the cost of the Korean war ($295 billion).'"

See also: Baker-Hamilton Report (2006), p. 27: "[…] the United States must expect significant 'tail costs' to come. Caring for veterans and replacing lost equipment will run into the hundreds of billions of dollars. Estimates run as high as $2 trillion for the final cost of the U.S. Involvement in Iraq."

143 Glanz, James: In Report to Congress, Oversight Officials Say Iraqi Rebuilding Falls Short of Goals. *New York Times*, October 31, 2007, www.nytimes.com/2007/10/31/world/middleeast/31reconstruct.html

See also: Baker-Hamilton Report (2006), p. 23, 57: "[…] about $34 billion to support the reconstruction of Iraq, of which about $21 billion has been appropriated for the 'Iraq Relief and Reconstruction Fund.' Nearly $16 billion has been spent […], Congress has little appetite for appropriating more funds for reconstruction. There is a substantial need for continued reconstruction in Iraq […]." "Recommendation […]: U.S. economic assistance should be increased to a level of $5 billion per year rather than being permitted to decline."

144 Aslan (2006), p. 78 et seq.

145 Aslan (2006), p. 84.

146 Goldziher, Ignaz, Vorlesungen über den Islam, 1963, p. 34, 309, cited from www.geistigenahrung.org/ftopic28531.html: "If he kills his ward he will not smell the scent of paradise. If he upsets his ward and gives him burdens too heavy to carry, I will be his accuser on judgment day … He who does injustice to a Christian or Jew will be accused by me." [Translation]

147 Hadithen des Imam Muslim Siddiqui, Abdul Hamid: Imam Muslim (202–261H). *Sunna.org*, www.sunnah.org/history/Scholars/Imam_muslim.htm

148 Sura 21:91: "And she who was chaste, therefore We breathed into her (something) of Our Spirit and made her and her son a token for (all) peoples."

149 Cited and agreed after a personal conversation with the author.

150 Sadrzadeh, Ali: Die entzauberte Revolution. *Qantara.de*, www.qantara.de/webcom/show_article.php/_c-468/_nr-79/i.html

151 Todenhöfer, Jürgen: Ein mit Dollar beladener Esel kommt weiter als jede Armee. *Süddeutsche Zeitung*, December 29, 2001, p. 14.

152 Haubold, Erhard: Das muslimische Asien wird radikaler. *Frankfurter Allgemeine Zeitung*, October 13, 2001, p. 2.

153 15 of the 9/11 perpetrators came from Saudi Arabia. The others came from Egypt, Lebanon and the United Arab Emirates.

See also: Unnamed author: The hijack suspects. *BBC News Online*, September 28, 2001, http://news.bbc.co.uk/2/hi/americas/1567815.stm: "Mohamed Atta, 33, possibly an Egyptian national, has emerged as a key link among the 19 men. He is believed to have been at the controls of Flight 11 when it hit the World Trade Center and has been linked to hijackers on two of the three other planes. Investigators say Atta was part of a terrorist cell in Hamburg, Germany, and received flight training in Florida. [...]"

154 Gellman, Barton; Ricks, Thomas E.: U.S. Concludes Bin Laden Escaped at Tora Bora Fight. *Washington Post*, April 17, 2002, p. A01.

155 Berking, Sabine: Mullah mit Motorrad. *Frankfurter Rundschau*, July 10, 2002, p. 15.

156 Schley, Nicole: Die Bush-Doktrin. Amerikanische Außenpolitik unter neuen Vorzeichen. *C.A.P. Europäische Zeitung*, September 1, 2002, www.cap-lmu.de

In addition: MacLeod, Scott: A Date With a Dangerous Mind. *Time*, September 25, 2006, p. 32: "[...]Ahmadinejad has also made rhetorical gestures of conciliation, sending an open letter to George W. Bush and inviting the U.S. president to a televised discussion about 'the ways of solving the problems of the international community.' (Bush ruled it out last week. 'I'm not going to meet with him,' he said at a White House news conference.)"

See also: Baker-Hamilton Report (2006), p. 46: "Violence cannot end unless dialogue begins, and the dialogue must involve those who wield power, not simply those who hold political office. The United States must try to talk directly to Grand Ayatolah Sistani and must consider appointing a high-level American Shia Muslim to serve as an emissary to him. The United States must also try to talk directly to Moqtada al-Sadr, to militia leaders, and to insurgent leaders. The United States can help facilitate contacts."

157 Schmidt, Helmut: Das Ethos des Politikers. Siebte Weltethos-Rede von Altbundeskanzler Helmut Schmidt, Tübingen, March 8, 2007. *Stiftung Weltethos*, www.weltethos.org/00--home/helmutschmidt-rede.htm: "A statesman who wants to serve peace has to take into considerartion the stateman on the opposite side; this means he has to speak to yesterday's enemy and tomorrow's possible enenmy. He has to listen and answer to him! Talk, listen and, if possible, compromise!" [Translation]

158 This notion refers originally to the Soviet Union. Halsall, Paul: Ronald Reagan: Evil Empire Speech, June 8, 1982. President Reagan: Speech to the House of Commons [London], June 8, 1982. *Modern History Sourcebook*. www.fordham.edu/halsall/mod/1982reagan1.html: "Must freedom wither in a quiet, deadening accommodation with totalitarian evil?" [Fordham University Sourcebook, New York, sees the origin of the word "evil empire" although not mentioned as such; Reagan refers in his London speech only to the evil of totalitarianism].

159 Sarkozy, Nicolas: Rede zur Eröffnung der 15. Botschafterkonferenz, Paris, August 27, 2007. *Botschaft-Frankreich.de*, www.botschaft-frankreich.de: "I am aware of the variables: I will no longer refer to them. I cannot tolerate an Iran that owns nuclear weapons and I want to emphasize France's determination in the present proceedings. We foresee increased sanctions, but also an opening if Iran dedides to follow its commitment. Only if we proceed this way will we succeed in escaping cathastrophic alternatives: Iranian bombs or bombing Iran. This fourth crisis, no doubt, is the most serious facing an international organization today." [Translation]

This position is reinforced later: Unnamed author: Sarkozy sieht Kriegsgefahr. *Focus*, December 12, 2007, www.focus.de/politik/ausland/iran_aid_229168.html: "Notwithstanding the last U.S. report on Teheran's nuclear policies, French President Nicolas Sarkozy speaks in public about the dangers of war with Iran. He is foremost concerned with Israel's security. [...] A U.S. intelligence agency concluded in a report published on December 3, [2007] that Iran had put its program to build nuclear weapons on ice by the end of 2003." [Translation]

160 Ebadi, Shirin (2007), p. 340.

161 C.f. MTL, Artikel KSZE: "The Helsinki Conference of July 3, 1973 [about security and co-

operation in Europe] with 33 European states (all except for Albania) as well as Canada and the USA. The second phase of the CSCE (Sept. 18, 1973 to July 21, 1975) in Geneva was dedicated to working out the final documents. The summit meeting in Helsinki (July 30 to Aug. 1, 1975) constituted the third phase of the CSCE. It ended with the signing of the last act of Helsinki. Ten principles were to lead the participating countries: 1) sovereign equality and the honoring of rights implied in sovereignity, 2) no threat or use of force, 3) sanctity of borders, 4) territorial integrity of states, 5) peaceful resolution of disputes, 6) non-interference in internal affairs, 7) honoring of human rights and basis liberties, 8) equality and right to self-determination, 9) cooperation between countries, 10) fulfilling of duties under international law, In addition, the last act provides trustbuilding measures in the field of military and cooperation in economics, science, technic, environment and other fields. [...]" [Translation]

162 Cited after a personal conversation with the author.

163 Church, Forrest: The American Creed. *The Nation*, August 29, 2002, www.thenation.com/doc/20020916/church

164 Todenhöfer, Jürgen: Das Wahnsinnsspiel. *Die Zeit*, August 4, 2005, p. 9.

165 nbu (author's initials): Die militärisch stärkste Nation. *Frankfurter Allgemeine Zeitung*, March 30, 2006, p. 7: "The U.S. is by far the strongest military power. In 2005 the military budget was 423 billion dollars. This is more than double the amount that all EU countries spend on their armies."

To compare Iran: nbu (author's initials): Die Krisenregionen der Welt. *Frankfurter Allgemeine Zeitung*, March 30, 2006, p. 7: "[Defense Expenditure] Iran 4.41 Billion Dollars, 420,000 soldiers) [...]."

Shah, Anup: World Military Spending. February 25, 2007, www.globalissues.org/Geopolitics/ArmsTrade/Spending.asp.

Comparable numbers in numerous countries, basis 2005 as well as estimates.

See also: Unnamed author: Iran's defense spending 'a fraction of Persian Gulf neighbors.' *GlobalSecurity.org*, May 31, 2006, www.globalsecurity.org/wmd/library/news/iran/2006/iran-060531rna03.htm: "Military Balance, published by the International Institute for Strategic Studies in London, puts Iran's defense budget for 2005 at $6.2 billion."

166 See: Afterword Endnote 48.

167 Hoffmann, Christiane: Sie kamen nicht bis Kerbela. *Frankfurter Allgemeine Zeitung*, October 21, 2006, p. 3.

168 Shultz, George P.; Perry, William J.; Kissinger, Henry A.; Nunn, Sam: A World Free of Nuclear Weapons. *Wall Street Journal* Op Ed., January 4, 2007, p. A15: "Nuclear weapons today present tremendous dangers, but also an historic opportunity. [...] reliance on nuclear weapons [...] is becoming increasingly hazardous and decreasingly effective. [...] John F. Kennedy, seeking to break the logjam on nuclear disarmament, said, 'The world was not meant to be a prison in which man awaits his execution.' [...] Ronald Reagan called for the abolishment of 'all nuclear weapons,' which he considered to be 'totally irrational, totally inhumane, good for nothing but killing, possibly destructive of life on earth and civilization.' Mikhail Gorbachev shared this vision [...]. The Non-Proliferation Treaty (NPT) envisioned the end of all nuclear weapons. It provides [...] that states that do possess them agree to divest themselves of these weapons over time. [...] Reagan and General Secretary Gorbachev aspired to accomplish more at the meeting in Reykjavik 20 years ago—the elimination of nuclear weapons altogether. [...] First and foremost is intensive work with leaders of the countries in possession of nuclear weapons to turn the goal of a world without nuclear weapons into a joint enterprise."

169 Author's conversation with Professor Dr. Walter Stützle, political scientist, journalist and former government secretary in the German Defense Ministry.

Bibliography

Aslan, Reza: *Kein Gott außer Gott. Der Glaube der Muslime von Muhammad bis zur Gegenwart.* München 2006

Baker, A. James III; Hamilton, Lee H. (2006): The Iraq Study Group Report. www.bakerinstitute. org/Pubs/iraqstudygroup_findings.pdf

Bedürftig, Friedemann: *Der Dreißigjährige Krieg. Ein Lexikon.* Darmstadt 2006

Bergen, Peter, L.: *The Osama bin Laden I Know. An Oral History of al Qaeda's Leader.* New York 2006

Bible, The. Ausgabe Neue Jerusalemer Bibel. Einheitsübersetzung. Mit dem Kommentar der Jerusalemer Bibel. Herausgegeben von Alfons Deissler, Anton Vögtle, Johannes M. Nützel. 13. Aufl., Freiburg i.Br. 1985

Bousselham, Hamid: *Quand la France Torturait en Algérie.* Rahma-Alger 2001

Carr, Caleb: *The Lessons of Terror. A History of Warfare Against Civilians.* New York 2002, Toronto 2003

Courrière, Yves: *La Guerre d'Algérie. Bd. 1: 1954–1957.* 2001

Ebadi, Shirin: *Mein Iran.* München 2007

Enzensberger, Hans Magnus: *Schreckens Männer. Versuch über den radikalen Verlierer.* Frankfurt/ Main 2006

Fanon, Frantz: *The Wretched of the Earth.* New York 2005

Ferro, Marc: *Le Livre Noir du Colonialisme.* 2004

Goethe, Johann Wolfgang (1961): *West-östlicher Divan.* In: *dtv Gesamtausgabe, Bd. 5,* München 1961

Grossman, David: *Lion's Honey: The Myth of Samson.* New York 2007

Jauffret, Jean-Charles: *Ces officiers qui ont dit non à la torture. Algérie 1954–1962.* Alger 2006

Kepel, Gilles: *Das Schwarzbuch des Dschihad. Aufstieg und Niedergang des Islamismus.* München 2004

Kepel, Gilles: *Die Neuen Kreuzzüge. Die Arabische Welt und die Zukunft des Westens.* München 2004

Bibliography

Kepel, Gilles; Milelli, Jean-Pierre (Eds.): *Al Qaeda in Its Own Words*. Cambridge, Mass. 2008

Koelbl, Susanne; Ihlau, Olaf: *Geliebtes, dunkles Land*. München 2007

Koran, The. Das heilige Buch des Islam. Translated by Max Henning, changed and revised by Murad Wilfried Hofmann. Kreuzlingen/München 2003

Küng, Hans: Spurensuche. Die Weltreligionen auf dem Weg. Bd. 2: Judentum, Christentum, Islam. München 2005

Küng, Hans; Senghaas, Dieter (Eds.): *Friedenspolitik. Ethnische Grundlagen internationaler Beziehungen*. München 2003

Le Cour Grandmaison, Olivier: *Coloniser. Exterminer. Sur la Guerre et l'État colonial*. Paris 2005

Maspero, François: *L'Honneur de Saint-Arnaud*. 1993

Nürnberger, Christian: *Die Bibel. Was man wirklich wissen muss. 3. Aufl.*, Berlin 2005

Rioux, Jean-Pierre: *La Torture*. In: Rioux, Jean-Pierre; Gervereaux, Laurent: *La France en guerre d'Algérie. Collection des publications de la Bibliothèque de documentation internationale contemporaine.* 1992, p. 92–99

Schwanitz, Wolfgang G. (Eds.): Germany and the Middle East. 1871–1945. Princeton 2004

Sorg, Eugen; Beck, Nathan: *Unbesiegbar. Reportagen*. München 2007

Sponeck, Hans-Christof: *Ein anderer Krieg. Das Sanktionsregime der UNO im Irak*. Hamburg 2005

Todenhöfer, Jürgen: *Wer weint schon um Abdul und Tanaya?* Freiburg i. Br. 2003

Todenhöfer, Jürgen: *Andy und Marwa*. München 2005

Ustinov, Peter: *Achtung! Vorurteile. Nach Gesprächen mit Harald Wieser und Jürgen Ritte*. Hamburg 2003

Zaidan, Amir M.A.: *At-Tafsir. Eine philologisch, islamologisch fundierte Erläuterung des Quran-Textes*. Offenbach 2000

Open Letter To His Holiness Pope Benedict XVI (by 38 Islamic authorities and scholars from around the world). *A Common Word*, October 13, 2006, www.acommonword.com

Response of over 300 leading Christian scholars to "Open Letter To His Holiness Pope Benedict XVI" as published in its entirety as a full-page advertisement in the *New York Times*, November 18, 2007, www.acommonword.com/lib/downloads/fullpageadbold18.pdf

Pope Benedict's Message to Prince Ghazi regarding A Common Word, November 27, 2007, www.acommonword.com/libdownloads/letter-from-the-vatican.pdf

About the Author

Dr. Jürgen Todenhöfer (68) has been an executive at a major European media group for more than 20 years. Before that he was a member of the German parliament for 18 years and spokesman for the CDU/CSU on development aid and arms control. He has written two bestsellers about the wars in Afghanistan and Iraq. With the royalties he established a children's home in Afghanistan and an HIV clinic for children in Congo. With the royalties from *Why Do You Kill? The Untold Story of The Iraqi Resistance* Todenhöfer is financing medical aid for seriously injured Iraqi refugee children and an Israeli-Palestinian reconciliation project in the Middle East.